The No-Nonsense Guide to Tornado Safety (2ⁿᵈ Edition)

Jeffery D. Sims

Books may be purchased by contacting the publisher and author at Lulu.com, Amazon.com, or contact the author at:

Beyond The Spectrum Books
http://beyond-the-political-spectrum.blogspot.com/

Cover Design: Jeffery D. Sims
Publisher: Lulu Books & Beyond The Spectrum Books
ISBN: 978-1-304-64864-8
1. Reference 2. Science 3. Weather 4. Safety 5. Tornadoes
Second Edition
Printed in North Carolina, USA

Acknowledgement

For Mom, Angela (Thank You), and my family (siblings, nieces, & nephews).

Table of Contents

The No-Nonsense Guide To Tornado Safety

Introduction

 Simply put, in some ways I was a normal child while in other ways, I was anything but. It is the abnormal part of my being which accounts for why you are holding this book in your hot little hands (or reading it on your tablet). While I enjoyed watching cartoons, reading comic books, and favored science-fiction (notice a pattern?), I was also fascinated—infatuated actually—with learning about strange, unusual, and otherwise unexplained uncommon events. Whether the subject was verifying the legitimacy of alleged occurrences explored in the field of parapsychology, learning about what things exist beyond the boundaries of our planet through the area of astronomy, or—of relevance to you the reader—understanding the causes of interesting weather phenomenon like tornadoes and hurricanes.

 As an adult, my love of learning had grown to encompass many other subjects, including history and politics (which I went to college to study). I had come to the awareness that I had/have an innate thirst for knowledge, about everything around me. As a result, I have more books than I will ever read, probably more than the average person. I've also probably had more different types of jobs than the average person. I've done a great deal of living. And in everything I've read, done, and observed, I've taken a great deal of awareness about life and the nature of the universe around us with me (yes, I know...a little grandiose, if not self-centered-sounding). I suppose by way of osmosis, I had also developed a love of teaching after having fallen into the vocation of substitute and adult education instructor. Because of these experiences, I have been driven to observe the world with an attempt to gain a deeper meaning of it all...and maybe bring a little bit of insight to others.

 I am also driven to write about my observations –without the latent bias of emotion, beliefs, or cultural beliefs—in order to convey a semblance of truth (the "teacher" in me I suppose) and maybe give others a little something to think about. This is why I started blogging and writing regularly some years ago. In an indirect way, writing is also a way for me to help others to think about and offer possible solutions to grander problems posed by counterproductive policies and our own individual thinking. But it was only recently that I was motivated to combine my proclivity for (objective) observation, thirst for learning, and ultimately my writing to create a series of books based on my own intellectual curiosities and love for seeking solutions to existing problems.

 This resulting compendium of interests and ideas has the (intended) benefit of imparting in those who chose to purchase and read it a level of awareness and knowledge about the an aspect of the dangers –those presented by the earth we live on—inherent in the world around us. And although there are no certain safe places to hide from real-life dangers, there *are* places as well as courses of actions that one can take to limit exposure to these dangers. I acknowledge this fact throughout the book(s) by using terms like *relatively*, *comparatively*, or variations of such words to convey that the suggestions offered are in, all likelihood based on research and other findings, the best options given the dangers and circumstances.

 It is my hope that the information in this book (or as I call it, "safety manual") will save a life, or at least prevent serious injury to those who would might be affected by a related dangerous experience.

 So without further ado, I present to you, the No-Nonsense Guide to Tornado Safety...

strong *squall line* (a line of thunderstorms that form along or ahead of a cold front) or among convective thunderstorms. Convective thunder-storms are storms that form during the heat of the afternoon within an area of atmospheric instability, and often form as a line of severe storms that generate a radar image known as a "bow echo" (see previous page). Torna-does that *do* form within these "quasi-linear convective systems" will form along the ends of these particular storm systems because this is usually where wind rota-tion and/or wind shear is most likely to to occur (however, there are always always be points all along the lines of these

TORNADO GENERATION

The severe thunderstorms called supercells provide the ideal spawning ground for tornadoes: Warm, moist air colliding with cool, dry air causes a swirling updraft that spins off tornadoes.

❶ Unstable conditions produce an updraft of warm, moist air

❷ As the air rises, varying wind speeds cause it to begin swirling; this is called a mesocyclone

❸ As the mesocyclone becomes more compact and intensifies, it may extend all the way to the ground in the form of a tornado

Overshooting top
Anvil
Anvil backshear
Supercell
Mesocyclone
Cumulonimbus clouds
Virga Rain that doesn't hit the ground
Wall cloud
Tornado
Hail
Rain
Direction of storm

A graphic illustrating the convergence of conditions necessary to form tornadoes

particular storm systems where rotation is strong enough to produce tornadoes within them). Torna-does that develop atypically at these points can form with very little or no warning. Essentially, there is a potential for tornadoes to form whenever warm and cool air masses collide.

While supercell and convective thunderstorms tend to produce the estimated 1,200 tornadoes that strike the U.S. yearly (primarily in the spring months), these storms can—and do—spawn tornadoes any time of the year that favorable conditions exist—including the generally colder winter months. Strictly speaking, unlike the time of year known as "hurricane season" (the time period of year in and around the U.S. when hurricanes are most likely to occur), there is no "tornado season" to speak of. However, for the sake of acknowledging their higher probability during certain times of the year, many meteorologists have dubbed the time of year that reflects the period when the U.S. sees the most regular tornado activity as "tornado season." Typically, the period beginning in mid-to late April through the month of June is when most tornadoes occur. The record for the most tornadoes in *any* month since record keeping began in 1950 was set in was set in May of 2003. There were a confirmed 543 tornadoes for that time period. The peak "tornado season" varies for different parts of the country depending on regular weather patterns (refer to the" Tornado Alley" portion under the "Where Do Tornadoes Occur" section).

Additionally, there is a lesser acknowledged but noticeably active "'second' tornado season" that begins around the first of November in the southern regions of the U.S. During this *second tornado season*, twisters tend to be more active in the area known as "Dixie Alley" (see the segment under the section "Where Do Tornadoes Occur" for more on this geographical and meteorological region). Both Tornado Alley and Dixie Alley represent regions of the U.S. where areas that experience the greatest level of climatic changes during the spring and autumn months. This is due to the fact that these seasons represent transitional periods in the climate, when masses of warm and cool air are more likely to collide and create the thunderstorms that spawn tornadoes

Although tornadoes typically form from (and during) thunderstorms, they can also be spawned from organized tropical weather systems—especially among the outer edges of these storms. Tornadoes that develop from tropical weather systems like hurricanes and tropical storms will most often form around the right quadrants of these storms. Tornadoes may also form ahead of such tropical systems along their course as they makes landfall (the point and time when such a storm moves ashore from the ocean).

There is a great deal of debate among meteorologists and others who study tornadoes as to what or *which* conditions (or single factor) cause tornadoes to dissipate. We know for certain is that tornadoes are fueled by a great deal of atmospheric instability and large scale air rotation. Constantly changing (as yet unidentified) atmospheric conditions in the vicinity of tornadoes and their supercell parents tend to cause varying levels of the duration and strength among and within particular storms. As such, tornadoes in can range in duration anywhere from a few seconds to as much as more than hour long. However, most last less than 10 minutes in duration. By the same set of conditions, as tornadoes travel along their often destructive paths, varying storm conditions within their parent storms can cause them to pick up strength and become more destructive.

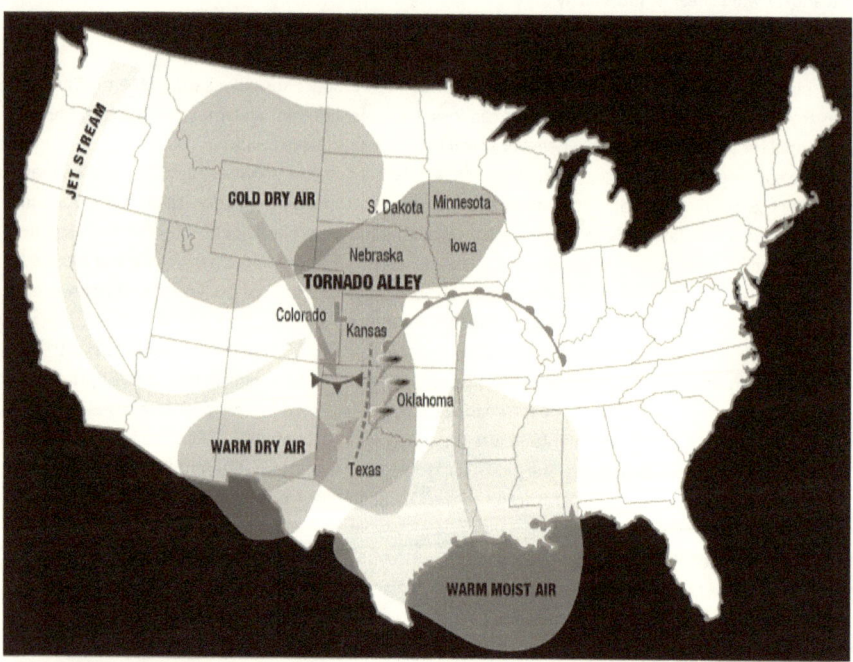

The above graphic illustrates the convergence of the various types of air masses that create the optimal conditions by which many-but not all-tornadoes form. Cool dry air moving down the eastern slopes of the Rockies warms and dries as it sinks onto the plains, creating a hot, dry zone free of any condensation clouds. During the heat of the day, warm dry air moves in from the desert Southwest. The resulting collision of air masses moves eastward and mixes with existing warm moist air ahead of it. If there is enough moisture and instability in the warm air, severe storms can form. It is under these conditions that severe storms can give way to supercell thunderstorms – the parent storm of tornadoes.

Table of Contents

Introduction

Simply put, in some ways I was a normal child while in other ways, I was anything but. It is the abnormal part of my being which accounts for why you are holding this book in your hot little hands (or reading it on your tablet). While I enjoyed watching cartoons, reading comic books, and favored science-fiction (notice a pattern?), I was also fascinated—infatuated actually—with learning about strange, unusual, and otherwise unexplained uncommon events. Whether the subject was verifying the legitimacy of alleged occurrences explored in the field of parapsychology, learning about what things exist beyond the boundaries of our planet through the area of astronomy, or—of relevance to you the reader—understanding the causes of interesting weather phenomenon like tornadoes and hurricanes.

As an adult, my love of learning had grown to encompass many other subjects, including history and politics (which I went to college to study). I had come to the awareness that I had/have an innate thirst for knowledge, about everything around me. As a result, I have more books than I will ever read, probably more than the average person. I've also probably had more different types of jobs than the average person. I've done a great deal of living. And in everything I've read, done, and observed, I've taken a great deal of awareness about life and the nature of the universe around us with me (yes, I know…a little grandiose, if not self-centered-sounding). I suppose by way of osmosis, I had also developed a love of teaching after having fallen into the vocation of substitute and adult education instructor. Because of these experiences, I have been driven to observe the world with an attempt to gain a deeper meaning of it all…and maybe bring a little bit of insight to others.

I am also driven to write about my observations –without the latent bias of emotion, beliefs, or cultural beliefs—in order to convey a semblance of truth (the "teacher" in me I suppose) and maybe give others a little something to think about. This is why I started blogging and writing regularly some years ago. In an indirect way, writing is also a way for me to help others to think about and offer possible solutions to grander problems posed by counterproductive policies and our own individual thinking. But it was only recently that I was motivated to combine my proclivity for (objective) observation, thirst for learning, and ultimately my writing to create a series of books based on my own intellectual curiosities and love for seeking solutions to existing problems.

This resulting compendium of interests and ideas has the (intended) benefit of imparting in those who chose to purchase and read it a level of awareness and knowledge about the an aspect of the dangers –those presented by the earth we live on—inherent in the world around us. And although there are no certain safe places to hide from real-life dangers, there *are* places as well as courses of actions that one can take to limit exposure to these dangers. I acknowledge this fact throughout the book(s) by using terms like *relatively*, *comparatively*, or variations of such words to convey that the suggestions offered are in, all likelihood based on research and other findings, the best options given the dangers and circumstances.

It is my hope that the information in this book (or as I call it, "safety manual") will save a life, or at least prevent serious injury to those who would might be affected by a related dangerous experience.

So without further ado, I present to you, the No-Nonsense Guide to Tornado Safety…

2

Tornadoes

What Are They?

Tornadoes—also called "twisters"—are nature's most violent storms. Though not everyone has actually seen a tornado, almost everyone knows what they look like, either by the way they are depicted in Hollywood movies, or by news footage of these destructive storms. A tornado is a violently rotating funnel-shaped column of (usually visible) air that extends from the clouds of a particular type of thunderstorm, to the ground. The actual funnel of a visible tornado is made up of condensed air, water droplets, dust and debris. The high speeds of a tornado's violently rotating winds are what make them particularly dangerous to both people and property, as they often can cause a great deal of damage, injuries, and deaths.

A tornado traveling across the Oklahoma landside (Photo courtesy of Daphne Zaras, NOAA)

How Do They Form?

Although the *exact* process by which that tornadoes form is not known, the process is known to involve a series of common (but not always present) meteor-ological phenomena, including the presence of *wind shear* (a change in wind speed and/or direction over a very small distance in the atmosphere), the convergences of cool moist air and warm humid air

A supercell thunderstorm photographed over the Midwestern U.S. (Montana).

in a given area, and localized temperature differences. But what we *do* know is that the majority of tornadoes are the extreme product of *supercell* thunderstorms. Supercell thunderstorms are a particular type of severe thunderstorm, characterized by the presence a rotating updraft of air in the

presence of strong *vertical* (as opposed to *horizontal*) wind shears. This vertical column of wind patterns begins to gradually narrow, and begins spinning with greater frequency and speed, becoming a fierce *mesocyclone*. As the present cool air drops, the present warm air rises. Under as-yet unknown precise conditions, the air be-gins rotating into a spiral and forms a *funnel cloud*.[1] If the wind rotation of a storm is strong enough, it is picked up on nearby weather radars, and authorities may issue a warning. The sky may turn an angry dark shade of green be-fore the characteristic funnel cloud forms. If the funnel of rotating air touches the ground, it becomes an actual *tornado*. Tornadoes generally form near the trailing edge of supercell thunderstorms. It is not uncommon to see clear, sunlit skies behind a tornado. On occasion— less than 20% of the time— tornadoes may form from either a particularly

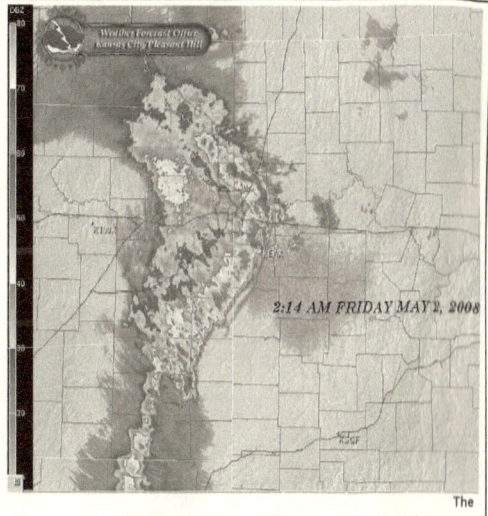

2:14 AM FRIDAY MAY 2, 2008

The radar image above illustrates the "bow echo" (because of its archer's bow shape) of a convective thunderstorm system as it appears on Doppler radar and news weather forecasts as it appears over the Kansas City Metropolitan Area in May of 2008. Because these weather systems can sometimes produce tornadoes, television viewers should be alert whenever such a weather system, particularly if it is categorized as "strong," approaches their area (Image courtesy of National Weather Service Kansas City).

---

[1] Mesocyclones do not always produce tornadoes. This fact is one of the mysterious and enduring aspects of meteorology which makes tornado prediction difficult.

strong *squall line* (a line of thunderstorms that form along or ahead of a cold front) or among convective thunderstorms. Convective thunder-storms are storms that form during the heat of the afternoon within an area of atmospheric instability, and often form as a line of severe storms that generate a radar image known as a "bow echo" (see previous page). Torna-does that *do* form within these "quasi-linear convective systems" will form along the ends of these particular storm systems because this is usually where wind rota-tion and/or wind shear is most likely to to occur (however, there are always always be points all along the lines of these

TORNADO GENERATION

The severe thunderstorms called supercells provide the ideal spawning ground for tornadoes: Warm, moist air colliding with cool, dry air causes a swirling updraft that spins off tornadoes.

❶ Unstable conditions produce an updraft of warm, moist air

❷ As the air rises, varying wind speeds cause it to begin swirling; this is called a mesocyclone

❸ As the mesocyclone becomes more compact and intensifies, it may extend all the way to the ground in the form of a tornado

Overshooting top
Anvil
Anvil backshear
Supercell
Mesocyclone
Cumulonimbus clouds
Virga
Rain that doesn't hit the ground
Wall cloud
Tornado
Hail
Rain
Direction of storm

A graphic illustrating the convergence of conditions necessary to form tornadoes

particular storm systems where rotation is strong enough to produce tornadoes within them). Torna-does that develop atypically at these points can form with very little or no warning. Essentially, there is a potential for tornadoes to form whenever warm and cool air masses collide.

While supercell and convective thunderstorms tend to produce the estimated 1,200 tornadoes that strike the U.S. yearly (primarily in the spring months), these storms can—and do—spawn tornadoes any time of the year that favorable conditions exist—including the generally colder winter months. Strictly speaking, unlike the time of year known as "hurricane season" (the time period of year in and around the U.S. when hurricanes are most likely to occur), there is no "tornado season" to speak of. However, for the sake of acknowledging their higher probability during certain times of the year, many meteorologists have dubbed the time of year that reflects the period when the U.S. sees the most regular tornado activity as "tornado season." Typically, the period beginning in mid-to late April through the month of June is when most tornadoes occur. The record for the most tornadoes in *any* month since record keeping began in 1950 was set in was set in May of 2003. There were a confirmed 543 tornadoes for that time period. The peak "tornado season" varies for different parts of the country depending on regular weather patterns (refer to the" Tornado Alley" portion under the "Where Do Tornadoes Occur" section).

Additionally, there is a lesser acknowledged but noticeably active "'second' tornado season" that begins around the first of November in the southern regions of the U.S. During this *second tornado season*, twisters tend to be more active in the area known as "Dixie Alley" (see the segment under the section "Where Do Tornadoes Occur" for more on this geographical and meteorological region). Both Tornado Alley and Dixie Alley represent regions of the U.S. where areas that experience the greatest level of climatic changes during the spring and autumn months. This is due to the fact that these seasons represent transitional periods in the climate, when masses of warm and cool air are more likely to collide and create the thunderstorms that spawn tornadoes

Although tornadoes typically form from (and during) thunderstorms, they can also be spawned from organized tropical weather systems—especially among the outer edges of these storms. Tornadoes that

develop from tropical weather systems like hurricanes and tropical storms will most often form around the right quadrants of these storms. Tornadoes may also form ahead of such tropical systems along their course as they makes landfall (the point and time when such a storm moves ashore from the ocean).

There is a great deal of debate among meteorologists and others who study tornadoes as to what or *which* conditions (or single factor) cause tornadoes to dissipate. We know for certain is that tornadoes are fueled by a great deal of atmospheric instability and large scale air rotation. Constantly changing (as yet unidentified) atmospheric conditions in the vicinity of tornadoes and their supercell parents tend to cause varying levels of the duration and strength among and within particular storms. As such, tornadoes in can range in duration anywhere from a few seconds to as much as more than hour long. However, most last less than 10 minutes in duration. By the same set of conditions, as tornadoes travel along their often destructive paths, varying storm conditions within their parent storms can cause them to pick up strength and become more destructive.

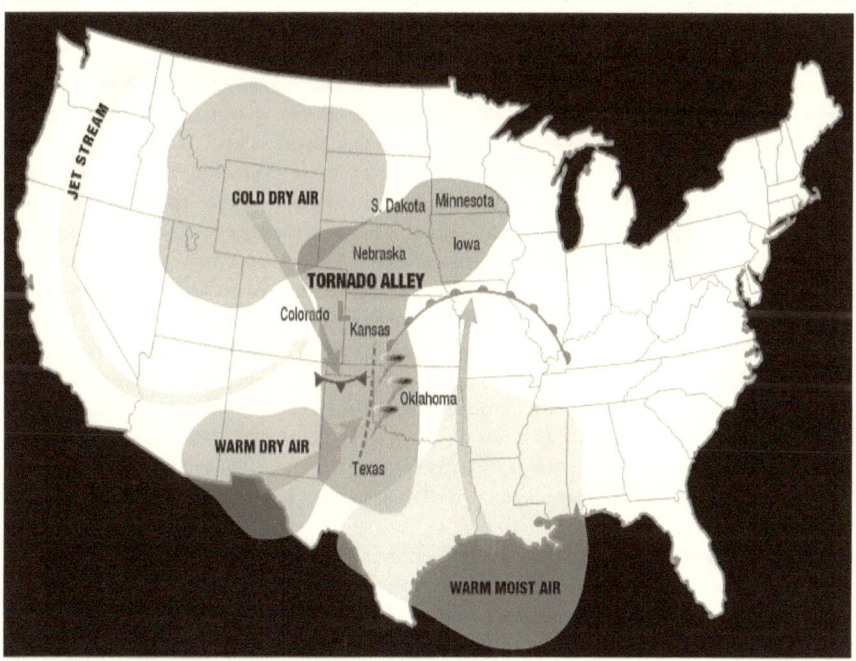

The above graphic illustrates the convergence of the various types of air masses that create the optimal conditions by which many-but not all-tornadoes form. Cool dry air moving down the eastern slopes of the Rockies warms and dries as it sinks onto the plains, creating a hot, dry zone free of any condensation clouds. During the heat of the day, warm dry air moves in from the desert Southwest. The resulting collision of air masses moves eastward and mixes with existing warm moist air ahead of it. If there is enough moisture and instability in the warm air, severe storms can form. It is under these conditions that severe storms can give way to supercell thunderstorms – the parent storm of tornadoes.

What Makes Them Dangerous?

Tornadoes are dangerous primarily because of their powerful and sometimes unpredictable winds. Recent research has determined that while some narrow-funnel tornadoes may comprise a single powerful wind vortex, many medium and larger tornadoes are actually made up of smaller vortices. In the case of these multiple vortex tornadoes, the winds of the larger funnel may only be strong enough to do minor damage to a particular structure as it passes over it. But one of the smaller embedded vortices, perhaps only a few dozen feet across, may strike the structure next to it with winds in excess of 200 miles per hour (more than 320 kilometers per hours), causing it to be completely destroyed[2]. The most powerful tornadoes are capable of even higher wind speeds. The May 3rd, 1999 tornado that tore a path through Oklahoma City, Oklahoma had wind speeds measured in excess of 301 mph (484 kp/h), the highest ever measured.

Because the winds and damage caused by tornadoes tend to vary from storm to storm—no two tornadoes are the same—meteorologists in the early 1970s devised a scale of measuring the strength of particular tornadoes. This scale was initially known as *The Fujita* (or "F") *Scale*, later revised in 2007 as the *Enhanced Fujita Scale* (or "EF Scale"), named after the pioneering tornado researcher Tetsuya Theodore "Ted" Fujita.[3] The EF Scale rates the strength of a particular tornado by assessing the amount of damage it causes after it has passed through a particular area, focusing mostly on the damage to physical structures. The winds from a tornado, even a relatively weak tornado (EF 0/EF1) can damage homes and buildings, as well as injure people. The strongest tornadoes (EF4/EF5) can, and often *do*

The Enhanced Fujita (EF) Scale				
EF Scale	Tornado Class	Wind Speed mph (km/h)	Description	
EF0	weak	65-85 (105-137)	Gale	- Peels off roofing shingles roofs; some damage to gutters or siding; broken tree branches; small trees pushed over.
EF1	weak	86-110 (138-177)	Moderate	- Roofs severely stripped; mobile homes damaged; loss of exterior doors; windows/glass broken.
EF2	strong	111-135 (178-217)	Significant	-Roofs sheared off; home foundations shifted; mobile homes completely destroyed; large trees snapped/uprooted; light objects projected; cars tossed.
EF3	strong	136-165 (218-266)	Severe	- Entire stories of well-constructed houses destroyed; severe damage to large buildings; trains overturned; trees debarked; heavy cars thrown through the air
EF4	violent	166-200 (267-322)	Devastating	- Well-constructed houses/whole frame houses completely leveled; cars thrown and small objects become lethal projectiles.
EF5	violent	> 200 > 322 (or greater)	Incredible	- Strong frame houses reduced to rubble and swept away; automobile-sized missiles fly through the air in excess of 100 m (109 yd); high-rise buildings have significant structural damage.

The Enhanced Fujita Scale, with revised parameters for damage determinations

[2] The inconsistent damage patterns caused by multiple-vortex tornadoes is the basis for the long-held belief that tornadoes "skipped" over houses or areas on the ground, before research proved the presences of this aspect of tornadoes.

[3] See the Appendix F for a brief biography and notable contributions of Ted Fujita to the field of tornado research.

lift vehicles, people, and even entire homes off their foundations. In some of the most violent tornadoes, bark has even been observed to have been stripped off large trees. Also in these most violent tornadoes, the destruction wrought can showcase exceptional damage-related phenomenon, such as heavy vehicles being flung great distances, straws being driven through tree trunks, and the very earth being stripped of grass and even pavement. However, EF4 and EF5-level tornadoes are not that common; statistically, they are less than 1% of all tornadoes that occur. Conversely, EF4 and EF5 tornadoes but make up the majority of total tornado deaths, hence their categorical nickname *violent* or *killer tornadoes*. The fact is that the majority of the tornadoes (80%) that occur in the U.S. in any given year are either EF0 or EF1-level storms. EF2 and EF3 make up the second most commonly-occurring level of tornadoes yearly (a little less than 20%). No matter the strength of a tornado, loose objects picked up and carried by the rotating winds can become potentially deadly missiles propelled with lethal velocity. Flying objects such as glass and wooden beams, propelled by high winds, as well as falling debris from damaged structures cause an *average* of 60-80 deaths a year the U.S.—the majority of deaths resulting from tornadoes.

During years when there is an unusual degree of high tornado activity, the U.S. death toll from these storms can be considerably higher. On April 3rd and 4th of 1974, an exceptional severe weather event occurred involving a then-unprecedented number of tornadoes at one time. Up until 2011, the so-called "Super Outbreak of 1974" was the largest tornado outbreak on record in a 24-hour period, for a concentrated region anywhere in the world. For 18 hours, beginning on April 3 and ending on April 4, 148 confirmed tornadoes struck in 13 U.S. states and the Canadian province of Ontario. So intense was this outbreak of tornadoes that a still-as-yet unprecedented number of 7 F5 and 23 F4 tornadoes were spawned. The 1974 outbreak resulted in a total loss of life of 319 people, some 6,000 injuries, and the damage and/or destruction of over 27,500 homes and structures. The 1974 tornado outbreak stood for as the costliest tornado-related event in terms of life and property damage for over 3 decades until the April 25-28 tornado outbreak of 2011. This tornado outbreak spawned some 358 tornadoes in 21 American states and regions of southern Canada, resulting in 324 deaths, and over $11 billion in property damage. Occasionally, there are comparatively smaller "tornado outbreaks," whereby a single weather system spawns multiple tornadoes over a particular region. The 1991 Andover, Kansas tornado outbreak was such an event, spawning some 55 tornadoes on April 26 of that year and resulting in 24 people in Kansas, Oklahoma, Texas, and Missouri.

Twin tornadoes over the American Plains in 2010.

Another characteristic of a tornado's unpredictability can be seen during particularly powerful supercell storms. Although infrequent, some tornado spawning supercell storms are capable of multi-funnel tornadoes. During these particularly powerful twisters, multiple-funnel clouds and/or tornadoes rotate around each other or travel as individual and separate funnels/tornadoes from the single storm. Typically, multiple funnel clouds are usually visible only early in a storm before they break

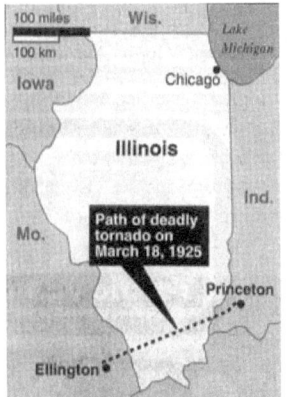

The path of the Tri-State Tornado.

off into individual tornadoes of their own. This usually occurs *only* after a supercell's circulation expands beyond a certain size and intensity, then it splits into two, or even three separate tornadoes from the "parent" tornado. Such a grouping separate individual tornadoes that split off from a single storm is sometimes called "satellite tornadoes." When multiple tornadoes occur over a larger area, but form individually from a single storm system, these are called a "tornado family." Multiple tornadoes can oftentimes be as destructive—if not more so—than a single powerful tornado.

Individually powerful tornadoes—those not related to tornado outbreaks—can cause an enormous amount of both property damage and loss of life under the right conditions. The Joplin, Missouri tornado of 2011, a catastrophic EF5-level storm, killed 158 people, injured 1,100, and caused an estimated $2.8 billion dollars in damage, making it the costliest single tornado in U.S. history (and among the 10 deadliest in the country's history). The Joplin tornado was the costliest single tornado in U.S. history; it wasn't by far the deadliest. The infamy of the deadliest single tornado in American history was the 1925 "Tri-State Tornado," so-called because this single tornado traveled a distance of some 219 miles (352 km) across 3 different states—Missouri, Illinois, and Indiana. The presumed EF5 (estimated because it occurred prior to the introduction of the Fujita Scale and tornado rankings) tornado killed 695 people across the stricken area, with most deaths occurring in the city of Murphysboro, Illinois—some 234 in total.

In addition to the dangers posed directly by the winds of tornadoes, other factors can and *do* occasionally make these storms even more dangerous, increasing the potential for death and destruction. One of these factors is the fact that some tornadoes can form very rapidly...so fast in fact that there may be warning at all. One such tornado occurred in February of 2012 in the small town of Wabaunsee, Kansas. According to one news report of the EF2 tornado, "the storm went from looking like a thunderstorm on one radar scan to showing a tornado in another scan four minutes later. On the next scan, the tornado was gone." Local radar had not indicated tornado rotation until the storm was directly over the town. By the time it had dissipated, 1 person was dead and 40% of the town was destroyed.

Not only can tornadoes form rapidly, but once formed they can move at unpredictable forward speeds and often travel in erratic patterns. Although the average forward speed of a tornado is between 25 - 40 mph (40 – 64 km/h), the forward speed of a tornado can not only vary from storm to storm, but also along the path of a particular tornado. Individual tornadoes can move along the landscape, often slowing downing or even remaining stationary, and then accelerate based on the varying power and strength of its host supercell. Some tornadoes have been observed to travel at speeds approaching 70 mph (more than 112 km/h). What's more is that although most tornadoes tend to travel in a southwesterly to northeasterly path, they have been known travel *any* direction—even changing course in mid-storm. These shifting patterns can make it difficult for people in the path of an approaching tornado to avoid being impacted directly from these storms, particularly if they find themselves out in the open. Moreover, the damage paths and duration of tornadoes can vary just as much in width as they do in strength and direction. The actual funnel of a tornado can be as narrow as several yards (meters) wide to several hundred yards/meters wide...or even wider. The widest (and largest) tornado on record was the EF5-rated El Reno, Oklahoma tornado of May of 2013. It was 2.5 miles (4.18 km) wide, traveled a total distance of 16.2 miles (26 km), and killed 18 people. And though a tornado can form for a little as a few seconds, most tornadoes only last between 10-15 minutes in duration. But as with strength, width, and direction, a tornado's duration can vary also as it travels across the ground. Some can last as long as an hour. The average distance a tornado travels is 4 miles (6.4 km), but may travel farther. The Tri-State Tornado of 1925 had the longest duration of any tornado on record; it was on the ground for 3.5 hours. [4]

Another inherent danger of tornadoes that can increase their overall threat potential is their visibility. *High-precipitation* (HP) supercell thunderstorms oftentimes produce rain-wrapped tornadoes, which make them very difficult to see. Approaching tornadoes can occasionally be hidden from view behind these heavy accompanying rains, often appearing to be simply heavy low-hanging clouds or a torrential cloudburst. Many tornado survivors have reported that had a very difficult time seeing an approaching tornado them because it hidden within a heavy rain curtain, not noticing the storm until it was right on right on top of them. Many motorists have in fact been killed by rain-wrapped tornadoes.

The time of day a tornado forms can make the difference between a few injuries and a great many fatalities. Most tornadoes occur in the late afternoon, usually between 3 and 9 pm. However, torna-does can strike at any time within a 24 hour period. And tornadoes that strike populated areas during periods of heavy pedestrian and/or vehicle traffic, so-called "rush hours," can be particularly dangerous—especially during traffic congestion. Vehicles can easily be picked up, tossed, and/or slammed to the ground (or against other solid objects) by tornado. Additionally, tornadoes striking at times of high pedestrian/vehicle traffic can invoke a level of fear in those who suddenly find themselves

endangered to the point where they will make counter-productive decisions. This is because most people caught out in the open or in public often do not know what to do in the event of an approaching tornado, resulting in panic and potential loss of life.

The image is all that the remains of a Ford Explorer pickup truck from the 2011 Smithville, Mississippi. According to witnesses the tornado hurled the SUV about ½ mile, into the town's water tower (the tower is in the image's background) and continued on another 1/4th of a mile (more than 402 meters) until impact. (Photo: Mississippi Emergency Management Agency).

---

[4] There is some speculation that the Tri-State tornado of 1925 was in fact a "tornado family" rather than a single twister. There is no definitive proof of this however.

Finally, nighttime and pre-dawn tornadoes are a particular danger because they occur at times when people are sleep, and are not as likely to hear making bad decisions that could cost them their lives. Tornadoes that strike after dark have the additional threat of visibility; they are harder to see. The only two ways to know of an approaching tornado during non-daylight hours are the characteristic loud roar of its winds, and the brief instances where the funnel against sky during flashes of lightening.

As a result of improvements in detecting, forecasting, and understanding the elemental components of tornado formation, the death rate from tornadoes overall has declined over the past century. But the decline in the nighttime tornado death rate has been slower, according to a 2008 study in the American Meteorological Society's journal "Weather and Forecasting." From 1950 to 2005, only 27% of tornadoes that occurred in the U.S. were nighttime of U.S. tornadoes. However, almost half of all tornado deaths were the result of nighttime tornadoes—42%. According to research, tornadoes striking from the period of midnight to sunrise were 2 and a-half times more likely to result in death and serious injury those than those occurring during other times within a 24-hour period. Combine that fact with a tornado's inherent unpredictability once it forms, the strength of its winds, and the ill-preparedness of those who might find themselves having to face the prospect one of these dangerous storms, and it's easy to understand why tornadoes are a force of nature that warrants concern.

The image of a nighttime tornado over the Texas countryside, captured by storm-chasers who were accompanied by a television news reporter and crew (courtesy of WHNT TV 19 in Huntsville, Alabama. May 16, 2013).

Where Do Tornadoes Occur?

Depending on where we live, tornadoes can be either a very real threat or an improbable abstract occurrence that happens *only* to those unfortunate people that we see on the news. Despite what one might think, tornadoes are a potential hazard no matter where we live. Tornadoes can (and do) occur in many parts of the world; on 6 of the 7 continents (excluding Antarctica) in fact. Outside of the U.S., Canada and Bangladesh tend to have the highest concentrations of tornadoes...but nowhere near as many as the U.S.

Similarly, in the U.S. tornadoes can strike anyplace. As a matter of history, they *have* been documented in all 50 states at some point. However, tornadoes are relatively rare in some parts of the U.S. States like Alaska and Washington may not experience a tornado within their borders for years. On the other end of the frequency spectrum, the state of Texas experiences the most tornadoes in any given year of any other U.S. state; it averages 139 tornado touch-downs annually. Some regions of the country as a whole are more prone exper-iencing tornadoes than others. The region *most* prone to the occurrence to tornadoes in the U.S. is located in the central part of the country. Meteor-ologists and those in the media have dubbed this geo-graphical region "Tornado Alley" for this reason—an area that includes the northern region of Texas, Okla-homa, Kansas, Nebraska, western Iowa, the east-ern edge of Colorado, South Dakota, and the

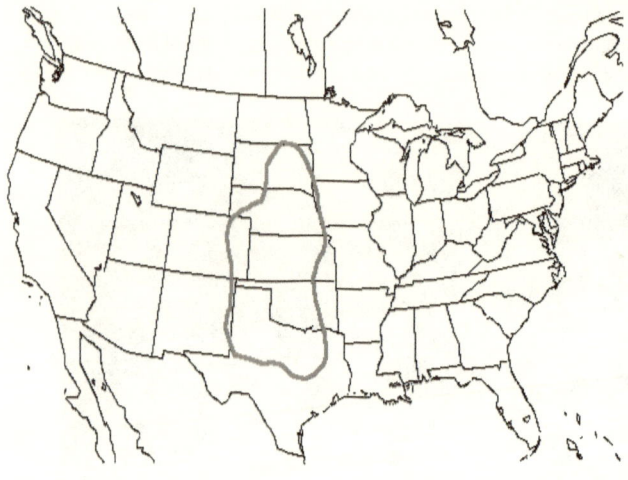

America's "Tornado Alley" region experiences the most tornadoes of any place on earth

southern edge of Minnesota (known as the Southern Plains of the U.S.). As previously hinted, tornado season for the Tornado Alley region begins in early April runs through May and into early June. In the Northern Plains and Upper Midwest, tornado season typically starts in June or July.

A secondary *tornado alley*, a region dubbed "Dixie Alley" refers to areas in the Deep South (encompassing the Gulf Coast, and the Southeastern U.S.) that are equally prone to the high occurrence to tornadoes. However, this region differs from the traditional Tornado Alley in several notable ways. The first distinction between Tornado Alley and Dixie Alley was revealed as a result of a recent study of climate and weather patterns. The research indicates that given certain unique weather patterns, certain regions of Dixie Alley might be *more* vulnerable to tornado strikes than regions within Tornado Alley itself. Another difference between these two regions of high tornado activity is that tornado season in Dixie Alley tends to begin experiencing *its* tornado season earlier (mid- to late April) in the spring than its more well-known sister region. What's more, the research indicates that tornadoes in this region of the country have a higher likelihood of being *long-lived* tornadoes—that is, tornadoes that remain on the ground longer than those occurring in other parts of the country. This is due in part to the earlier start of tornado season for this part of the country, when the atmosphere spawns more long-lasting and faster-moving tornadoes. This region is also more likely to experience tornadoes during the winter months. The winter time tornado outbreak of 2008 was the best example of these cold season storms that tend to occur in Dixie Alley. The so-called "Super Tuesday Tornado Outbreak" of that year began on February 5—the "Super Tuesday" when many states were holding primary elections for the then-upcoming presidential election—and continued through to the 6th. The result of the 2-day tornado rampage through Dixie Alley was a shocking 57 deaths from the 87 conformed tornadoes that affected 5 states.

Dixie Alley is a particularly dangerous for those who might find themselves facing an approaching tornado because of the nature of housing in the region. For one thing, the Southeastern part of the U.S. has the highest concentration of trailer park (manufactured) homes in the entire country. These particular structures are far more vulnerable to the damage a tornado can inflict than traditional studier-built structures with foundations. The winds in and near a weak or moderate strength tornado (or even a strong thunderstorm) might cause only roof damage to a more sturdy-built traditional home, but demolish or roll over a comparatively lighter weight mobile home due to its weaker construction and lack of a permanent foundation. For this reason, mobile homes—next to automobiles in some cases—are the

most dangerous place a person can be in a tornado. From 2000 to 2008, nearly half of deaths resulting from tornadoes occurred in mobile homes. In addition, most homes in this region of the country lack basements or similar underground spaces where study after study has shown to be the safest places to be in a tornado. Because of the higher-levels of humidity and warmer temperatures that can maintain instability well after dark, Dixie Alley tends to have a higher frequency of nighttime and rain-wrapped tornadoes, both of which are more difficult to visually see for previously-discussed reasons. Finally, the topography of the land in this region makes tornadoes that form here more dangerous. The terrain within this region is rife with hills, mountains, and an abundance of heavy vegetation such as trees...all which make it difficult to see an oncoming tornado coming in this region of the country (in the flat plains, people can see tornados coming from farther away).

What to Be On the Alert for...

Tornadoes, despite their overall destructive potential possess an almost countless number of individual characteristics. For example, some tornadoes may be spawned from intense supercell thunderstorms over a given geographical area. In some instances, the anticipated volatile atmospheric conditions which create the environment for these particularly strong storms to form can take a few days to assemble; this allows forecasters to sometimes issue severe weather advisories 1 or 2 days ahead of these conditions coming together —yielding a level of some predictability.

In other instances, tornadoes might spring up from fast-building thunderstorms that form during the heat of a late spring, early summer day, often giving no warning at all of their approach. Additionally, visible tornadoes have been observed to come in all kinds of shapes and sizes; narrow rope-shaped columns, mile-wide wedge-shaped monsters, and barely-visible condensation clouds are the various ways in which tornadoes have appeared. And those obscured by rain or lack of a visible condensation funnel can vary just as well, with nothing more than swirling debris clouds or the sudden manifestation of incredible winds in the immediate vicinity to mark their presence.

Despite their varying individual characteristics, any tornado can potentially threaten both life and property. Because of this fact, weather researchers have improved our general understanding of the conditions leading up to the formation of tornadoes. And although nothing can stop a tornado from damaging or destroying property, being alert for conditions and indicators of a potential tornado can mitigate how much of a threat these dangerous storms can be to human life.

The first step involves keeping aware of weather forecasts, and being on the alert for the potential for severe weather (most tornado-related deaths and injuries happen to people who are unaware and uninformed during existing tornado conditions). Whenever weather conditions favor the potential for tornadoes to form—particularly in and around areas of intensifying thunderstorms—the National Weather Service (NWS) or its satellites offices around the country will issue weather bulletins. These bulletins are then sent to various local and national news outlets, which then people living in an area that might be affected by tornado-favorable conditions should be alert for changing and/or dangerous weather conditions. These weather alerts are issued over radio, television, and the internet in the form of *tornado watches* and *tornado warnings*.

A Tornado Watch issued by the NWS is an alert to the public indicating that conditions exist for the possible formation of tornadoes within a given geographical area. In such rare cases (between 3% - 7% of all weather forecasts), the NWS will issue what is known as a "particularly dangerous situation" (PDS). In the case of tornadoes, a *PDS tornado watch* implies that there is an enhanced or very favorable risk of either multiple violent tornadoes (EF2-EF3) or powerful or long-lived tornadoes (EF4 – EF5) forming in a given area. During these times, individuals in the watch area should be on the lookout for changing weather conditions—especially as these conditions relate to oncoming and sudden severe weather (e.g., high winds, ominous-looking cloud formations, lightening, torrential rains, etc.).

The NWS will issue a Tornado Warning whenever either a tornado or funnel cloud is actually sighted, or when Doppler radar returns indicates the signature strong wind rotation (indicating a possible forming tornado). Although it does not mean that a tornado is *assured* to strike one's particular location, it is usually issued because a tornado (or impending tornado) is in the vicinity and provides high-probability alert for those living in the warning area. In a few rare instances, a "tornado emergency" will be issued by the NWS. Tornado emergencies are used to warn the public of an active, particularly dangerous, and long-lived potential tornadoes in a given area. The National Weather Service has a protocol—based on tangible criteria—which are used when issuing a tornado emergency:

> In exceedingly rare situations, when a severe threat to human life and catastrophic damage from a tornado is imminent or ongoing, the forecaster may use the terminology "TORNADO EMERGENCY FOR [GEOGRAPHIC AREA]" … this terminology should only be used when reliable sources confirm a tornado, or there is clear radar evidence of the existence of a damaging tornado such as the observation of debris.[5]

When a tornado warning is issued, it is highly advisable to seek shelter and enact any previously crafted tornado emergency procedures. Be aware of changing weather conditions in the warning (or watch) area. Although every tornado is unique unto itself, many of these violent windstorms have exhibited tell-tale patterns prior to their arrival. Based on past observations from both weather experts and tornado survivors, weather-related indicators of a possible imminent tornado include the following:

1. Falling hail (large ice pellets) is common before many—but not all—tornadoes. In some instances, intense hail and rain can visually obscure approaching tornadoes from being seen. In other cases, there may be no hail at all prior to a tornado. However, hail is not always an indicator of an impending tornado.
2. A sickly greenish or greenish black color to the sky (the green indicates the presence of hail).
3. Although most people usually think that tornadoes are associated with raging winds and deafening thunderous noise, this isn't always the case. Many times a tornado will be precipitated by quiet and stillness. A strange stillness of the air, resulting in an "unusual quiet" has often been described as having been experienced before (and sometimes after) a tornado.
4. Many municipalities within the U.S. have warning sirens installed around populated areas to warn of weather emergencies (or other potential disasters). These sirens are often sounded when a tornado is either in the area or has been sighted. This is the best indicator to seek shelter and/or enact tornado emergency plans.
5. Very fast-moving clouds, especially those moving in a rotating pattern or converging toward one area of the sky. Additionally, an approaching cloud of debris oftentimes precipitates the arrival of a tornado…even without a visible funnel. At this point, there is usually very little time left to find safety. Cover should be sought immediately.
6. A loud roaring sound that becomes more pronounced. The sound of a tornado has been compared to that of a jet engine, a rushing waterfall, and/or railroad train at close range. This is the sound of the wind from the condensation funnel of a twister as it approaches. Contact is imminent at this point.
7. Debris dropping from the sky. This is an indication that the tornado's condensation funnel is nearby
8. The familiar "funnel-shaped" of the condensation funnel. Depending on terrain of where the funnel column travels, a tornado may be difference in appearance and/or color. For example, a tornado that travels over areas of the American Great Plains may pick up huge amounts of dust

---

[5] Patrick T. Marsh, "A Review of NWS Tornado Emergencies," National Weather Service Instruction (NWSI), 19 April, 2012:4-6.

and dirt, forming a brownish-red color. Condensation funnels that pick up little or no debris can appear gray to white in color. When a tornado travels over a body of water (known as a *waterspout*), they can turn very white or even blue. Finally, tornadoes that form dry environments can be nearly invisible, marked only by swirling debris at the base of the funnel.

9. At night, tornadoes are often illuminated by frequent lightning. Their distinct funnel shape can often be seen against the lightning flashes. In addition to the roar of a tornado's winds, another way to spot a tornado occurring after dark is a consistent flash of electricity caused by falling and snapping of electrical power lines as the wind funnel passes over and destroys utility poles and electrical transformers.

The No-Nonsense Guide To Tornado Safety

How to Prepare In The Event Of a Tornado...

Be proactive! You and/or every member of your family should have a prepared plan of action—or at the least a clear understanding—in order to know what to do in the event of an emergency, in this case a tornado threat. Every course of action related to an emergency plan should be based on advanced preparation and foresight of anticipated needs if there is a disruption in day-to-day functions of a community.

Understand Your Tornado Risk
The level of preparedness should be in proportion to the actual risk for tornadoes. Those who live in say, west of the Rocky Mountains in the U.S. would not be expected to be as cognizant to the risk of tornadoes as those living to the east. And while it should be reiterated that tornadoes can potentially strike anywhere and anytime the conditions exist, those living in Tornado and Dixie Alleys should be *the* most prepared...especially for the possibility of stronger tornadoes. In addition, tornadoes can be spawned from hurricanes, tropical storms, and tropical depressions in and around the (Southern) coastal regions where they come ashore. However, despite the violent nature of a tropical storm or hurricane, the tornadoes they spawn tend to be weaker than those produced by non-tropical thunderstorms. Those affected by such storms need to be aware of this possibility and plan accordingly.

In addition to the need to understand the seasonal, climatic, and geographical risks associated with the probability for tornadoes, individuals need to be aware of the risk for tornadoes when the actual conditions for their formation are present. As a result of advancements made in weather research, technology, and the proliferation of weather-detecting radars, weather forecasters have gotten better over the last several decades at anticipating whenever conditions for tornado formation are likely to come together. In some instances, forecasters can anticipate the likelihood for favorable tornado conditions days in advance, giving those living in such affected areas time to plan ahead in the event of a worse-case scenario. However, predicting *exactly* when and where a tornado will form is still beyond the scope of weather forecasting.

This is why many amateur and professional *storm chasers* risk serious injury and even death hunting down, documenting, and studying tornadoes across the U.S. every year. Storm chasers are a group of individuals who are either paid or volunteer to observe and study extreme weather phenomena,

Famed and longtime storm chaser and researcher Tim Samaras was noted for not taking unnecessary risks while tracking tornadoes throughout America. And despite being one of the premiere storm hunters in the field of meteorology, his years of experience, his expertise, and the precautions he would take while researching tornadoes were not enough to ensure his safety. On May 31st, 2013, Samaras along with 2 other storm chasers were killed while following the El Reno, Oklahoma tornado.

especially tornadoes, in order to learn as much about these storms as they can so that calculating their behavior, and eventually their predictability becomes a reality.

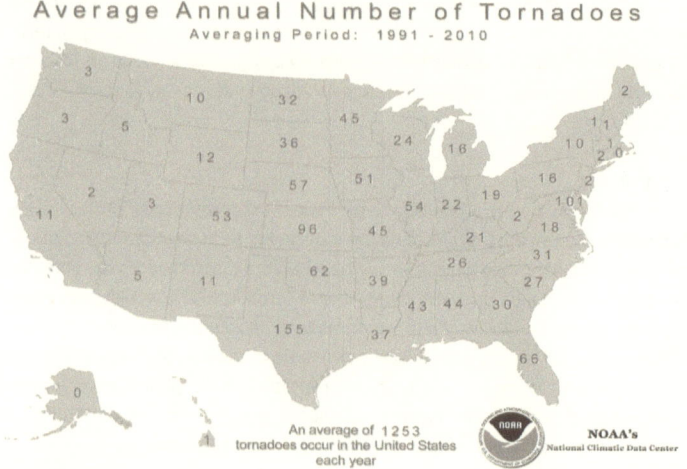

Average Annual Number of Tornadoes
Averaging Period: 1991 - 2010

An average of 1 2 5 3 tornadoes occur in the United States each year

NOAA's
National Climatic Data Center

The map above is the *average* annual number of tornadoes each state has for the most recent 20-year period (Courtesy: National Oceanic and Atmospheric Administration).

Still, with the advent of *Doppler radar* (a radar system that utilizes microwave pulses to measure both distance and velocity of winds within storms),   forecasters are often able to "see "areas of rotation in approaching storms that may indicate the beginnings of a forming tornado even before the funnel is even visible. On weather radar, tornadoes usually—but not always—are indicated by the presence of a "hook echo" on weather radars.

Additionally during these alert periods, the NWS activates *weather spotters*, certified individuals whose job is to visually confirm dangerous weather conditions. Weather spotters are trained to notice or "spot" danger-ous weather conditions like tornadoes or indications that one might be in the process of forming, such as a funnel cloud, a rotating wall cloud, etc. Should they actually spot any of these phenomena, they are responsible for contacting the nearest NWS office and/or emergency personnel such as law enforcement so that a tornado warning to the public. Spotters are the NWS' official *eyes on the ground* who gives visual confirmation of a tornado on the off-chance that a near-by Doppler radar Doppler radar may not indicate the presence of an actual tornado on the ground.

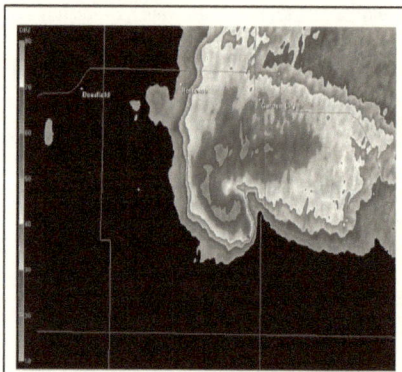

The characteristic "hook echo" of a tornado on Doppler (the various colors represent wind intensities within the storm).

During periods when weather forecasters are advising the public of changing and/or deteriorating conditions, it is both prudent and important to monitor the various media outlets for weather advisories. Most media will interrupt regular programming in the event of any type of serious weather emergency such as a tornado. For this reason it is usually a good idea to keep either a radio or television on in the background of the home (or business), to be monitored periodically for alerts. Another option, particularly for schools and other places of business, is to have a designated person monitor weather-related news on the internet. There are many news local news websites that are updated up-to-the-minute insofar as weather forecasts and weather alerts. Moreover , there are just as many national (and international) websites that focus strictly on providing weather forecasts and alerts, some with downloadable applications that provide real-time weather conditions for a given region. Some of these sites offer e-mail and text alerts that go directly to cell phone users to alert them of adverse weather conditions.[6] Lastly, special types of radios known as *weather alert radios* (also known as *weather radios*) can be purchased for constant monitoring of weather conditions. When plugged in, these radios scan and monitor weather broadcasts by the National Oceanic and Atmospheric Administration (NOAA) for emergency weather information. During times of adverse weather conditions, these radios will broadcast an alarm and a subsequent watch or warning for an affected area to warn residents of weather-related dangers.

For the most part, the risk that someone might experience a tornado is based on a set of complex yet generally predictable variables. In many cases, weather forecasters are able to anticipate when weather patterns that create an increased risk for tornadoes are likely to come together as much as 48 hours in advance. Tornado watches will be issues when there is an increased chance for storms that might spawn a tornado. The likelihood that any given area might experience a tornado will wax or wane depending on the annual frequency of tornadoes such an area is prone to experiencing, the particular weather patterns of the season, and pretty much the luck of the draw. But if by circumstance these individual variables converge, it's best to be aware that the potential for a destructive tornado to form is present.

Plan Your Shelter

First know that any building can be damaged by a strong enough tornado. This potentially includes even skyscrapers if it struck head-on by say, a powerful EF5 tornado. But for the most part, larger studier-built structures like skyscrapers fare typically better at withstanding catastrophic or even severe structural damage from a tornado. This is because their steel-reinforced frames lack the load-bearing wall design that smaller structures like homes have (which makes homes more vulnerable to collapse due to the winds of a tornado). The overall good news is that *most* grounded structures offer some measure of shelter against all but the strongest tornadoes--and even an EF5 tornado is survivable under some circumstances. It is for this reason that buildings and homes are where those seeking to escape death and/or injury from tornadoes should seek shelter.

Everyone, and that includes individual members of a family should be aware of the safest place in a dwelling in which to relocate to in the event of an approaching tornado. In homes that have them, basements or storm cellars are the safest places to gather. Because they are underground, basements

---

[6] See Appendix D for a list of weather-related computer and smart-phone applications.

and cellars provide protection from both the powerful winds of a tornado as well as flying debris. Those seeking shelter in a basement should seek additional cover under a sturdy workbench, billiard table, or heavy furniture to protect themselves from falling debris. Additional cover is important because in the most violent of tornadoes, the open area in a basement may not provide enough protection. Sometimes the floor of a home either collapses or is swept away; allowing debris can then be thrown into the basement. These positions of additional cover should not be located under heavy furniture or appliances located on the floor above them. If no such fixtures are not available—and if time permits—a mattress can be taken into the basement and used to cover the body for additional protection.

If personal safety factors more than financial savings, another option for homes without basements or storm cellars is to construct a tornado-proof "safe room." A safe room is a fortified hardened structure, normally built as a separate area either inside or below (i.e., underground) a residential dwelling or other type of building, similar to a traditional storm cellar. Constructed from heavily reinforcing materials and anchored securely to a building's foundation, safe rooms—in times of threatening weather –provide the occupants of a home or building a safe place to seek shelter from the deadly effects of a tornado. Although most safe rooms are built as separate areas from the rest of a dwelling, such as a designated area of a garage, in some instances normal–use rooms within a home, such as a bathroom or closet can retrofitted to serve the same purpose. Home- or business-owners might either opt build a safe room themselves (assuming competent execution), hire a construction firm, or contract companies that specialize in the installation of these hardened structures in and around

homes. In the absence of a basement, safe rooms are specially constructed to withstand the high winds of a tornado. More to the point, safe rooms are built to withstand both, the high-velocity flying debris driven by a twister's fierce winds as well as the high-velocity flying debris driven by a storm's fierce winds as well as the direct impact of tornadoes them-selves.

A large of piece of wind-driven wood pierces an asphalt parking lot barrier, damage from the 2011 Joplin, Missouri EF5 tornado.

Figure. 1.1   Figure. 1.2

Above: The construction of a tornado "safe room" by a construction company (Fig. 1.1). Safe rooms can be installed underground in most homes, but in areas where the lay of the ground doesn't permit such a placement, they can be installed inside an existing dwelling—with a minimum loss of effectiveness. Figure 1.2 is an example of how a well-constructed safe room can stand up in the aftermath of a powerful tornado.

However, because the average strength, frequency, and likelihood of tornadoes vary from region to region, safe rooms are not all constructed the same. The building standards for the construction of an effective safe room in the U.S. are outlined by the Federal Emergency Management Agency, better known as FEMA.[7] According to FEMA standards, for a safe room to function at the optimum level of intent commensurate with the threat, these special shelters should be constructed to provide protection based on the criteria of "near-absolute protection" in the event of such natural disasters like a tornado. This means that the criteria for building a safe room, its strength and effectiveness in the event of a tornado will vary along with the threat potential. For example, the requirements for building a safe room built inside a home in the middle of *tornado alley*, where the frequency and strength of a tornado is greater than most other regions of the country, will greater than one built in a summer home near Bangor, Maine—where tornadoes are far less probable.

The major advantage of these safe rooms is that even if the rest of dwelling becomes severely damaged or destroyed, safe rooms provide "near-absolute protection" in extreme weather events, including tornadoes and hurricanes (see the unit on hurricanes). The biggest disadvantage is cost. Installing a safe room can be prohibitively costly for many both home- and building-owners (starting at $2,000 for the most basic model and more for more secure and models. These costs can be mitigated if home-owners opt to build the room themselves, saving money in labor (however, such an endeavor has

---

[7] FEMA is an agency arm of the United States Department of Homeland Security. Created in 1978, the agency's primary purpose is to coordinate resource and logistical responses to disasters that have occurred in the United States, and where the efforts and resources of local and state agencies are overwhelmed. FEMA is also responsible is responsible for programs that take action before a disaster, in order to identify risks and reduce injuries, loss of property, and recovery time. The agency has major analysis programs for floods, hurricanes, dams, and earthquakes, and provides these services for territories of the United States, such as Puerto Rico and Guam. The governor of the state in which the disaster occurs must declare a state of emergency and formally request from the president that FEMA and the federal government respond to the disaster.

its own advantages and disadvantages). But there *are* government-sponsored programs that offer the opportunity to apply for grants at the local, county, and state levels. These grants, for the most part, are funded through federal block grants to the various levels of government, and help defray the cost of

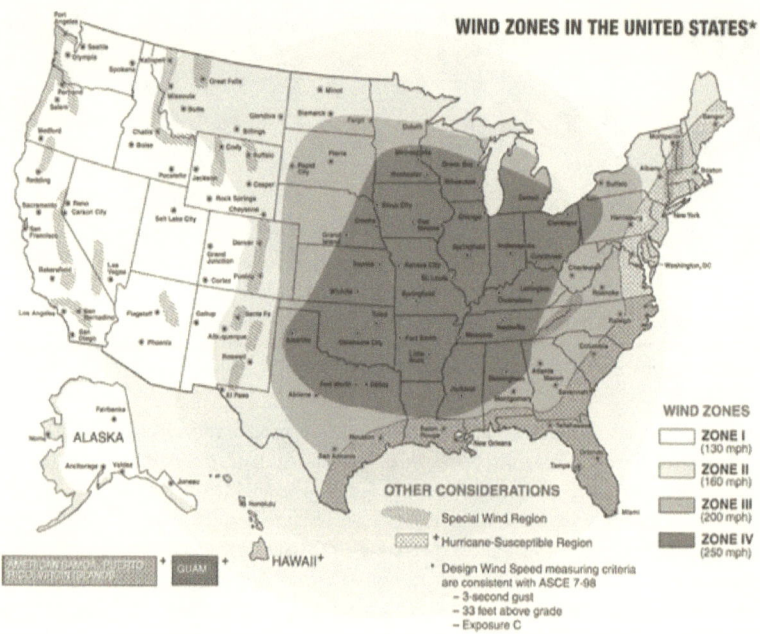

WIND ZONES IN THE UNITED STATES*

OTHER CONSIDERATIONS

Special Wind Region

* Hurricane-Susceptible Region

* Design Wind Speed measuring criteria
are consistent with ASCE 7-98
— 3-second gust
— 33 feet above grade
— Exposure C

WIND ZONES

ZONE I
(130 mph)

ZONE II
(160 mph)

ZONE III
(200 mph)

ZONE IV
(250 mph)

FEMA standards for the construction of tornado "safe rooms" are based on the average frequency and strength of tornadoes for different regions of the country. Each "wind zone" represents the suggested maximum level of protection that safe rooms built within them should provide occupants.

building tornado-proof safe rooms for both family dwellings and other important buildings such as schools.

Planning ahead in securing shelter in the event of tornado is probably the biggest single factor in increasing survival. Even if a home or building has no safe room or basement itself, occupants could make an agreement with a nearby home-owner or neighbor who *does* have a basement or safe room. In the event of a tornado, neighbors or businesses with basements or safe rooms could agree to take in others nearby who are seeking shelter from an approaching tornado. Indeed, some communities across America have designated community tornado shelters where nearby neighbors can go from an approaching tornado.[8] More and more trailer parks are installing these types of community shelters as well.

---

[8] See Appendix E in the rear of the book for a list of known community tornado shelters nearest in the U.S.

But in the case of tornadoes, many homes simply do not have safe rooms. Similarly, many areas of the U.S., particularly those in the South and the West do not have basements (for reasons based on a combination of economics, culture, geography, and the ground topography of these regions). This is true, even in the nation's two *tornado alleys*. For those living in such dwellings in these regions, the safest place to take shelter is on the lowest level/floor in the building, in an enclosed room without windows. The best rooms for protection are those located in the center of the dwelling (again on its lowest level), such as a space underneath a stairwell, in an *interior* hallway, a closet, or in a bathroom. The goal is to place is for individuals to place as many walls (i.e., barriers) between themselves and the winds of a tornado outside the dwelling to limit the chance of contact with flying debris—the primary cause of injury and death in tornadoes (rooms adjacent to the outside of the home may not offer enough protection, especially from flying objects that can easily penetrate a single wall). In seeking shelter in such enclosed spaces, individuals should protect themselves further from injury with the added protection of some sort of padding. It should be a part of the overall proactive shelter plan to take an available mattress or some other form of padding (like multiple heavy blankets) into the protective space.

If forced to seek shelter in an *interior* bathroom, the best way to maximize protection from falling objects and high-velocity wind-driven projectiles is by lying down in the bathtub and covering the body (as an aside note, interior bathrooms have an added measure of safety—especially in older homes—in that metal pipes between the rooms tend to provide a level of bracing for the walls). Again, padded coverings of some type taken into the bathroom will add further protection. If there is no time to reach for covering, the head should be covered with the hands to protect this vital part of the body with the hands as much as possible.

However, levels of both discretion and caution should be applied in determining whether or not to seek shelter in a home without an underground dwelling. Some tornadoes, particularly the most powerful EF4 and EF5 tornadoes—on rare occasions—are so violent that survivability chances for those not able to take shelter underground are low. In fact, many weather experts say that the most powerful tornadoes (those with winds in excess of 200 mph/321.87 km/h) are simply "not survivable" unless shelter is sought underground. In such a scenario, it might be more advisable—if possible and if the tornado is far enough away—to get into a vehicle and attempt to drive in a direction out of the path of the approaching storm.[9]

For those living in an apartment building, pre-planning is an essential part of reducing injury and/or possible death from a tornado. If there a tornado warning has been issued or one is known to be in the area, those living on an upper floor should get to the lowest level of the building immediately. This could be an underground parking garage or a neighbor's first floor apartment. The same applies to those residing in a high-rise apartment building. However, many tornadoes often form and strike with very little warning. If there isn't enough time to get to a lower level, the best option is to seek shelter in an

---

[9] In most cases, an automobile is potentially *the* most dangerous place to be in a tornado. However, when faced with a life-or-death decision such as attempting to ride out the most powerful type of tornado above ground, or attempting to drive out of its path, the individual must chose the option that best increases the chances for survival based on the particular circumstances. The forward speed of tornadoes can vary, with the highest observed being around 73 mph (117 km/h). In theory, cars can travel faster than tornadoes (based on the highest forward speed observed to this point, but this doesn't mean that tornadoes cannot travel faster. Nevertheless, it *is* possible to drive out of the path of an approaching tornado—if the option is available—by driving at right angles to the tornado's oncoming path. Although the majority of tornadoes tend to travel in a southwesterly to northeasterly path, keep in mind though that tornadoes can often change direction as they travels across the landside.

enclosed area, such as the hallway in the center of the building, away from windows. Just as in a home without a basement, other relatively safer locations include a closet or a bathroom.

Most places of public accommodation such as office and municipal buildings, hospitals, schools, and factories not only have designated shelter areas in the event of emergencies such as tornadoes, but routinely have protocols in place such as warning systems to make patrons aware of threatening or changing conditions. Also, many publicly-assessable places such as schools and places or employment tend to hold occasional drills to limit confusion in the event of such emergencies. In most cases, it is very important that the precautionary steps illustrated and practiced during drills are followed in the event of a tornado-related emergency in order to limit the potential for panic, injury, and/or death. However, in the uncommon event that such protocols are not in place, the precautions are much like those in most other dwellings. Occupants should head for an enclosed, windowless area in the center of the building—*away from glass* and on the lowest floor possible. Interior stairwells are an ideal location in a building such as a skyscraper or other large building (additionally, stairwells have the added benefit of allowing for a quick rout to the lowest level of the building). Large open rooms with wide-span and/or flat roofs such as cafeterias, gymnasiums, auditoriums, and shopping centers should be avoided, as their particular style of construction almost ensures a potentially lethal collapse of heavy debris and building material on those seeking shelter in such rooms. Once inside a relatively safer location, oc-

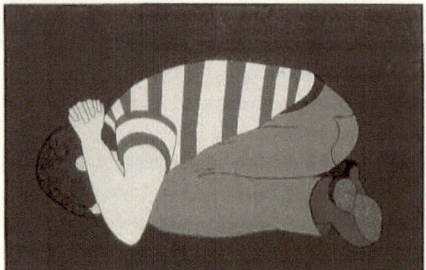

The ideal position to place the body in the event of a tornado, protecting vital areas like the head with the hands.

cupants should get as low to the floor as possible by assuming a position of protection, covering the head with the hands or some form of protection. As a precaution, elevators should also be avoided as much as possible, as someone could be trapped in them should the power supply to the building is disrupted.

Because tornadoes can form unexpectedly, it's quite possible that people patronizing businesses or other public venues like shopping centers, banks, churches, and theaters can be caught totally unawares, away from more familiar surroundings when a tornado develops. In such an instance, customers should follow a variation of the same general safety procedures. This involves seeking out the best area of safety within the structure, which is (still) the most interior enclosed area within the structure—while continuing to avoid windows and rooms that are parallel to the outside walls. If possible, move quickly but orderly to an interior bathroom or hallway. In some cases, this might entail seeking shelter in unusual—but still relatively safe—locations. There are instances where individuals have survived particularly powerful tornadoes by taking shelter in such makeshift places as bank vaults in banks, storage and walk-in freezers in restaurants and stores, and underneath interior stairwells in other publicly-assessable buildings...dwellings that were all-but completely obliterated after a passing twister. In many of these cases, the only portion of the buildings left standing were the very areas where people sought shelter from the tornadoes. Wherever shelter is sough, individuals should crouch down and assume the position of protection (see the image on the previous page) to increase protection against falling debris.

The popularity of outdoor activities as well as the need to travel between places of work and leisure means that eventually, one might find themselves outdoors during threatening weather. And the rules for those caught outside in an urban environment as different for those caught in rural areas. If caught driving in a city or urban area, and a tornado alert is issued (or when weather conditions are noticed to be deteriorating to the point where a tornado suspected to be nearby), traffic and the lay of the roadway tends to limit a driver's maneuverability so often the best choice is to find a secure building and take refuge. in an urban environment, shelter should be sought inside the nearest sturdy building.

However, it possible to encounter a tornado and there is no a safe building around, such as when one is driving on the open road in more rural areas. With regard to such an instance, the NWS's official safety guidelines for preventing serious injury (and the possibility of death) have been consistent since the 1970s. The NWS advises against attempting to outrun a tornado in a vehicle, or staying in the vehicle at all. But the individual circumstances of a particular crisis situation might force deviation from conventional wisdom. For example, if in cornered in a vehicle during an approaching tornado, it might be possible to maneuver from the direct path of the twister.

But the best option among a few bad options is based on statistically decreasing the likelihood of immediate death and/or injury by limiting exposure to wind-driven flying projectiles—the chief cause of tornado deaths. The best choice is to lie flat and face-down on low ground, preferably in some type of indentation in the earth such as a ditch or a hole in order to limit exposure to flying objects at just-above ground-level. Once low to the ground, one should protect the back of the head with the arms (a variation of the position of protection). If possible, this course of action should be taken away from the vicinity of nearby trees, cars, or other objects that might otherwise be picked up and hurled on top of those comparatively fragile human bodies forced to seek shelter by lying on the ground.[10]

Because tornadoes can both form and/or move very quickly in the vicinity of drivers, there may not even be time for at-risk drivers to abandon an automobile and seek shelter low to the ground. Reacting to this level of threat by a tornado is another unfortunate instance of playing the odds of survival and major injury-prevention among limited choices. It is because of this observation that the National Red Cross recently changed its tornado safety guidelines regarding the option of a car versus ditch as a

---

[10] The choice of getting out of get out of the car and into a ditch during an approaching tornado requires a context of informed decision-making. This is an option of last resort that comes with its own set of risks, just as attempting to out-maneuver a tornado in a vehicle. The hazards of getting out of the car and into a ditch during a tornado include: being struck by flying debris and large hail stones (possibly with lethal force) before seeking a position of safety; heavy rains that often accompany supercell thunderstorms may flood nearby ditches and indentations, producing a drowning threat (particularly if you are pinned down by debris; being struck by lightning; and actually being picked up and thrown by a tornado's funnel should it travel directly over the point on the ground where an individual is seeking to avoid being impacted by flying projectiles and wind. This is an option that has had some measure of success in the past for those who have sought it, but its effectiveness is highly reliant to some degree on a measure of chance and circumstances. On May 31st, 2013 Oklahoma City tornado resulted in 9 deaths, with 7 dying in their vehicles as they sought to drive away from the path of the oncoming tornado. The local interstate that residents were using to escape the oncoming tornado became jammed with cars, trapping drivers in the path of the oncoming storm.

refuge against an oncoming tornado. According to the Red Cross, if getting out of the vehicle and seeking shelter on the ground below the level of the dangerous winds is not possible, a "reasonable" course of action may be to stay in the automobile and take advantage of its metal frame and safety glass (both of these materials might offer some level shielding from the strong winds and flying debris). Along with an automobile's constructed material, seat belts and air bags might add some protection to a vehicles occupant (s) if the vehicle is overturned or tossed by the winds. The vehicles occupants (s) should remain in their seatbelts, while ducking their below the window line of the vehicle.[11] In the scenarios involving seeking shelter from an approaching tornado while out in the open and away from the relative safety of stable buildings, individuals should consider the individual variables of their particular situation. It should be noted that attempting to outmaneuver in an automobile and getting out and seeking shelter in a low indentation in the earth both have their individual set of risks that might be overwhelming in different instances (discussed in more detail in the following section). Given that it is virtually impossible to outrun an approaching tornado on foot, the options must be weighed based on the situation and circumstances at hand, and the best course of action(s) most likely to result in the *least* amount of injury and/or death should be considered.

Tornadoes are potentially nature's most destructive natural disaster, based partially on their overall unpredictability and propensity to strike in populated areas (although many occur in open fields and large expanses of unpopulated areas as well). The bottom line is that although there are no guaranteed "safe" places to be in a tornado, planning and talking shelter can increase the odds of survival and/or reduce the likelihood of personal injury. The reality is that that there only a few places of "absolute" safety in a tornado, including professionally designed underground storm and in-home shelters. Pre-tornado planning and precautions are simply meant to improve your chances of survival, but don't guarantee it.

What To Avoid

Just as there are precautions that one can take to limit injury and death in the event of a tornado, there are actions and decisions that one can make which may put one more in jeopardy, thus increasing risk to life and limb. While some of these bad decisions are being effectively countered by new research

---

[11] Just as in the case of seeking shelter in a ditch from a tornado if out in the open, the negative option of remaining in an automobile also requires a context of informed decision-making. This is also an option of last resort that comes with a set of risks. The hazards of remaining in a vehicle during a tornado include: the very real possibility that flying debris may penetrate the vehicle and strike those seeking shelter in it; the vehicle may be become an airborne projectile, be rolled, or tossed by the (the strongest) tornado, injuring or crushing the occupants; occupants can be sucked out by a tornado's winds if not secured within the vehicle. Like seeking shelter in a ditch, this is an option has had a mixed measure of success in the past. However, at times the risks for injury and/or death tend to outweigh the intent of using the vehicle as an impromptu shelter in a tornado. On May 31st, 2013, a series of powerful tornadoes struck the Oklahoma City, Oklahoma area, resulting in several deaths. In one case, an entire family drowned as the drainage ditch they sought shelter in from an approaching tornado quickly filled with water and swept them away. During the same series of Oklahoma tornadoes, a weather reporter and storm chaser (as well as several aides) for The Weather Channel cable network videotaped their own encounter with one of the twisters while attempting to document the destruction in one of the network's vehicles. Footage showed the weighty sport utility vehicle and its passengers being suddenly overtaken by one of the funnels and being blown and tossed off the road some 200 yards (182 meters). The occupants could be heard being told to put their heads down below the window-level of the vehicle. The occupants of the vehicle all walked away with minor injuries.
The option of remaining in the vehicle during an approaching tornado is not without its credible supporters. In 2009, suggested changes in tornado safety guidelines regarding automobiles were based "research led by Kent State University professor Tom Schmidlin that found that a relatively small percentage of vehicles were moved or tipped over during tornadoes and that a vehicle may be safer than the outdoors."*Despite this change in stance by the Red Cross on the issue of staying inside a vehicle, the NWS still maintains that more traditional advice of abandoning the vehicle in favor of laying on the ground out of the above-ground wind patterns. Individuals who might find themselves in such an unfortunate circumstance must weigh the individual factors of their predicament and make the best informed-decision.

and understanding of a tornado's effects, others reflect the stubbornness of long-held myths and beliefs related to tornadoes that—despite newly-generated research and an evolving understanding of them—refuse to die.

- Mobile homes are one of the worst—if not *the* worst—place to be in a tornado. Because of comparatively weaker construction, mobile homes are far more vulnerable to being totally destroyed than grounded, more permanent structures. Their light weight makes then highly susceptible to being overturned and destroyed by the strong winds of powerful thunderstorms as well as tornadoes. Even mobile homes with a tie-down system cannot withstand tornado-force winds. If you live in a mobile home, being proactive with a tornado contingency plan is the best measure to prevent major injury or loss of life. *Do not stay in a mobile home!* Leaving a mobile home and heading to a nearby building (preferably one with a basement) is the best course of action. If there is no shelter nearby, consider—depending on the circumstances—either getting into an automobile and attempting to outmaneuver the tornado, or leaving the mobile home and lying flat in a low portion of ground (e.g., a ditch, ravine, or culvert) and shield your head with your hands.

- For years, it was an accepted belief that if motorists encountered a tornado while driving on a highway, pulling over and taking shelter under a highway overpass was the prescribed course of action. Much of this belief was bolstered by news footage of drivers stopping their vehicles and doing just *that*...taking shelter under a nearby overpass in the midst of an approaching tornado. *Do not seek shelter under an overpass!* Research has shown that taking shelter under an overpass can actually increase the probability of injury and/or death due to the *wind-tunnel effect*—the increase in the force and velocity of winds when they are forced through a narrow area. This means that if a tornado were to pass directly over an overpass in which someone has taken shelter underneath, instead of offering protection against the twister's winds, the confined space of the tends to increase wind speeds...and the potential danger. This is because a person seeking shelter at the top of an overpass could encounter the higher wind speeds (and more high-velocity debris) at elevated levels above the ground. This actually *increases* the chance a person can even sucked out or carried away from the overpass by the fierce tornado winds. These destructive winds also produce airborne debris that are blown into and channeled under the overpass at higher speeds, increasing the likelihood that someone seeking shelter under an overpass will be injured or killed by these flying objects. If driving out on the open road or a highway, decisions must be quickly made on how best to avoid injury and/or death. In order of the preferred options in a bad situation, the *best* course of action is to shelter in a sturdy, well-constructed building. If this is not possible, the occupants of the vehicle may have to consider abandoning it to lie flat in a ditch or ravine, while clasping the hands behind the head for protection from flying debris. In the event that neither of these options aren't possible, it might be necessary to stay in the vehicle with the seatbelt buckled. With this option, the head should be placed down below the windows and the head covered with the hands (a blanket, jacket, or other type of additional protection might be used in conjunction with these actions). Vehicles and lying flat in a ditch/low to the ground are options of last resort, as overpasses offer NO PROTECTION from tornadoes and should not be used as sheltering areas.

- Up until more recent times, it was thought that the damage to homes and buildings caused by tornadoes was due to rapid changes in the air pressure between the inside and the outside of the dwelling (i.e., that houses "explodes" from changes in air pressure). Because of this, it was thought that opening all of the windows in a house before a tornado would reduce damage by equalizing the pressure between the inside and outside the structure. The fact is that homes are damaged by the powerful winds produced by a tornado, not by the changes in the air pressure. If a tornado is approaching, *do not waste time opening window!* The time one would waste opening windows would be better served seeking shelter. Taking the time to open all windows not only will fail to protect the dwelling from the powerful winds, but puts occupants— especially the one opening windows—at risk from flying glass and other wind-driven shrapnel.
- If located in a high-rise or other type of multi-story dwelling during an approaching tornado, *do not use the elevator to reach the lower floors!* There's a good chance that the power to buildings might be lost. If that happens, anyone attempting to reach the lower floors in an elevator might become trapped in a non-functioning elevator. In addition, the stairwell—the preferred method of escape to lower floors—tend to be structurally reinforced, offering a greater measure of stability *and* protection should a tornado strike while evacuating.
- Do not assume that you will know what to do in the event of a tornado! Plan ahead! Former President Abraham Lincoln once said, "If I had eight hours to chop down a tree, I'd spend six hours sharpening my ax." This thought should be kept in mind when preparing for weather safety. The point is that time (and effort) should be put into tornado preparation, as a way of saving precious time reacting blindly in the unfortunate event that one might actually be forced encounter these destructive storms. Plans of action prevent one from being caught off-guard not knowing what to do should a tornado-related crisis arises.

Build a disaster/tornado supply kit

In the event of a disaster such as a tornado, emergency first-responders might have a difficult time reaching those affected. In worst-case scenarios, a particularly powerful tornado or expansive storm system might level both homes *and* businesses in a town or city...and therefore needed supplies might not be available for purchase after a storm has passed. Basic services that such as water, electricity, gasoline, and maybe even phones might be disrupted, perhaps for extended periods of time. The best way to confront the possibility of such disruptions is by planning to have a "disaster kit" handy just in case.

A disaster kit is a collection of supplies and basic items which might be needed in the event of a tornado or similar disaster, the purpose of which is to assist in survival until either the crisis has passed, or until help arrives. These kits can be purchased either online or in some brick-and-mortar stores, prepackaged with most anticipated essentials. The prices of these prepackaged disaster kits will vary, depending on how stocked they are with supplies. Some pre-packaged kits contain basic supplies such as first aid kits, bottled water, and flashlights. The more expensive deluxe kits might include extra amenities such as a small portable toilet and/or water purification tablets in the event that the water supply is disrupted. However, effective disaster kits can just as easily be created by purchasing anticipated items individually, collecting and storing them in a designated tornado shelter. Once purchased or gathered together, emergency items should be stored in a container of some type, such as a moderate-sized plastic tote or foot locker capable of being sealed or closed for protection.

An example of the type of plastic tote (with a sealed lid) which can be used to store a tornado disaster kit. A footlocker of approximately the same size would be just as effective a storage location.

At the very least, an effective disaster kit should include the following:

Clothing & Bedding:

- An extra change of clothing. In a few some cases, the clothing worn by those who might be directly impacted by a disaster like a tornado can become drenched with rainwater, torn, or otherwise lost during a disaster like a tornado. An extra change of clothing for every person anticipated to take cover in the shelter is a reasonable precaution to take in the face of such a possibility. An extra change of clothing should include both underwear and foot in the event of maximum need.
- Waterproof rain ponchos, in the event that a change of clothing might not be practical. Rain ponchos serve the same purpose as an extra change of clothing, especially considering that weather often remains **inclement after a tornado has passed.**
- Several blankets, preferably one for every person anticipated to take cover in the shelter. Blankets can provide an extra measure of warmth in the event of falling temperatures (which sometimes happens after a major tornado outbreak, especially those that occur in the winter months). In addition to providing warmth, blankets can be folded into impromptu padded sleeping surfaces in the case of extended need. For the extra expense sleeping bags can be purchased in lieu of blankets, however, blankets are more practical and can be utilized for more multiple purposes in the event of an emergency.
- Two pairs of sturdy work or safety gloves. Oftentimes, scattered debris and other structural pilings end up strewn across the immediate areas of structures where people seek shelter during a tornado, particular those that have sustained a direct hit. In removing these obstructions, a sturdy pair of gloves would protect the hands from sharp edges and other potentially dangerous objects while moving trying to evacuate from damaged structures.

The No-Nonsense Guide To Tornado Safety

Foodstuffs:

- A 2-3 day supply of non-perishable, no refrigeration-required food should be packed away somewhere inside or near the shelter itself in the event of loss of power. Additionally, the foods selected for storage should be of the type that are tightly sealed, and requires very little or no preparation (i.e., cooking) and/or need for water. Ideally, food products with similarly close expiration dates should be purchased and stored together, so as to make replacing them at the same time easier if they expire before use.
  If storage space availability is limited, consider purchasing military-style Meals Ready to Eat (MRE) packet from surplus or camping stores. MREs are small packets of food rations that require just a little water or maybe some heat to prepare. And in the case of individuals who feel that they *must* have heat-prepared food, consider packing away "canned heat." Canned heat is a concentrated source of cooking heat which is designed to be burned directly from its canned casing as an emergency source of heat for the limited cooking of food (it can be found in most camping stores). For foods that don't require cooking, keep track of their individual expiration dates.
- Canned meats such as tuna and beef (jerky) have extended storage lives, so such items should be a main staple of any stored food (unless there are vegetarians present, in which case canned vegetables should be included).
- High energy food sources such as protein, energy, and/or granola bars are idea for storage. They require less space than canned foods, even those that don't require preparation.
- Bottled water. Stored in sealed plastic bottles, bottle water keeps amazingly well for extended periods. The U.S. Food and Drug Administration (FDA) estimates that most bottled water has a potentially indefinite shelf life, so replacing drinking water to maintain its availability in case of emergency use should not be a major concern. Ideally, one gallon of water per person, per day should be stored for emergencies. However, Nursing and/or pregnant women, children, and individuals with pre-existing medical conditions might need more water.
- Canned juices, milk, and/or soup (milk and soup can be purchased in powered form, and as such tend to have long shelf lives. Extra water should be considered if powdered foods are going to be used).
- Crackers, cookies, and other ready-to-eat snack foods add variety as well as supplement the food supply.

Supplies/Communication:

- Waterproof matches, lighters, and/or candles (preferably those that come contained in a semi-enclosed glass holder to prevent the flame from being extinguished) for a source of light in the event of the loss of power. Alternatives to flame-based illumination to consider (in the event that gas leaks from exposed or damaged gas lines might create an explosive hazard) include a rechargeable flashlight or penlight, or long-period glow sticks
- A battery-powered radio for keeping updated on vital information or instructions. A better alternative might be to consider purchasing one of the types of portable radios that rely on

neither batteries nor electricity. These units are powered by cranking a handle, which charges a miniature generator inside the unit enough to power it *without* batteries or electricity for a limited amount of time.

- An all-purpose toolkit, or a multi-tool such as a heavy-duty Swiss army knife or Weatherman multi-purpose instrument. Tools and other such implements can be invaluable in the event that there is a need to clear debris and other obstructions from areas of protection and blocked evacuation paths leading from shelters.
- A non-electric/hand-powered can-opener (if not a function of a multi-purpose tool).
- A pack of batteries, preferably an assorted pack containing multiple sizes for battery-powered instruments (e.g., radio).
- Plastic utensils, paper plates, and/or Tupperware or plastic containers (with lids) for serving food.
- Sanitation supplies, in the event that any assistance is not immediate and facilities are not immediately available. A stock of sanitation supplies that includes toilet paper/towelettes, liquid bottled soap or detergent, a 5-gallon bucket with a lid, plastic garbage bags with ties, a disinfectant, a strong cleaner such as bleach, and personal hygiene items should be sufficient to lessen the hardships of extended periods without access to facilities.
- A first-aid kit. First-aid kits of varying degrees of items can be purchased at mostly any "big box" store, or can be created from scratch based on anticipated needs. At the very least, an effective first-aid kit should contain bandages (the plastic adhesive, rolled cloth, and/or the "liquid" varieties), roller cloth bandages, sterile gauze pads, towelette wipes, medical tape, a liquid antiseptic (e.g., alcohol and/or peroxide), anti-bacterial soap, smelling salts, petroleum jelly, latex gloves, tweezers, scissors, a thermometer, and aspirin or some other pain-reliever.
- A whistle or some other type of noise-maker. Oftentimes, individuals taking shelter from an approaching tornado can find themselves trapped underneath debris or collapsed structures that have been directly impacted. First-responders often have a difficult time in trying to locate these individuals, especially in the evening and nighttime hours. Being able to signal your location by way of a noise-maker could make the difference between being immediately rescued and spending an extended period of time being counted amount the missing.
- A small, portable electric generator, in the event that electrical power is lost due to downed electrical wires.

Additionally, it may be a good idea to purchase a small metal lockbox, a safe, or some manner of highly resistant-to-damage container. The purpose of such an item is to store important papers and documents such as financial records, insurance papers, and birth certificates. Even without the threat of tornadoes destroying a home, it's a good idea to keep such documents stored in damage-resistant containers anyway to avoid their loss from other significant threats such as a house fire or a flood.

After A Tornado

The best-case scenario deriving from a tornado emergency is that the storm doesn't directly impact either life or property. But in the unfortunate event that a home or community *is* struck by a tornado, the first priority afterwards should be a headcount and welfare check of those present in the area of sought-after safety (i.e., shelter). After ensuring that all occupants of a shelter area are accounted for, everyone should quickly but calmly leave the shelter area to seek assistance.

There may be some injuries to those in shelter areas. If so, and depending on the type and severity of injuries, it will be imperative to secure medical assistance. Protecting one's self and others requires promptly treating any injuries suffered during the storm and using extreme care to avoid further hazards. If available, a first-aid kit (preferably one is available in a disaster/emergency kit) may be used to stabilize or address any minor wounds before evacuating those in need of assistance (on the assumption that the injuries aren't *too* severe).

Injuries related to tornadoes may result from the direct effects of the twister, or it may occur afterward when people walk among debris and enter damaged buildings. In many instances, a significant amount of injuries stemming from a tornado striking a populated area occur after a tornado has passed—many happening during rescue attempts, cleanup, and other post-tornado activities. Among the types of injuries that happen in a tornado's wake are those resulting from coming into contact with protruding (and sharp) objects such as nails, cuts from broken glass, and electrocutions from stepping on fallen electrical lines.

Because tornadoes often damage power lines, gas lines, or electrical systems, there is a risk of fire, electrocution, or an explosion so caution be utilized when entering any or exiting structure that has been damaged. Do not touch downed power lines or objects in contact with downed lines. Report any electrical hazards to the police, the fire department, or to a public utility or other emergency worker. If possible, wear sturdy footwear, long sleeves, and gloves when handling or walking on or near debris.

Those affected by a tornado should monitor their battery-powered radios or televisions for both emergency information and reporting of resulting hazards. Battery-powered lanterns and/or flashlights sources of light should the electrical powered be non-functional. Candles are the next best source of light in such situations. If candles are to be used, they should be in safe holders away from flammable items.

Avoid the use of generators, grills, camp stoves, or other gasoline, propane, natural gas, or charcoal-burning devices in an enclosed area. Such areas include as the room in a home, a basement, garage, or camper—or even outside near an open window, door, or vent. Using such apparatuses inside of enclosed areas could result in a buildup of carbon monoxide (CO). Carbon Monoxide is an odorless, colorless gas that can cause sudden illness and death if allowed to build up in enclosed areas for an extended period of time.

Finally, property owners, renters, and businesses affected by tornado damage should contact their insurance companies and/or the appropriate insurance agents. Insurance personnel should be given as complete a list as possible of any items damaged or destroyed by the tornado.[12] Items damaged should not be disposed of until insurance adjusters have had a chance to view them.

---

[12] It is always a good idea beforehand to make a detailed list of the most important items in a home, apartment, or business for insurance purposes, to be kept and maintained in a secure place with other important records. It's an even better idea to make a photographic or videotape record of these items as well as the condition of property prior to any damage and/or destruction. At any rate, those affected by tornado damage should be prepared to answer questions about the severity and extent of damage. See appendix for more relevant information regarding insurance coverage for tornado damage.

And depending on where one lives, resources will usually begin marshaling immediately in tornado-damaged areas. In cities and urban areas, the response for assistance—medical, financial, and charitable—is typically faster, usually within a few hours. In more remote regions, assistance can take considerably longer, depending on the level of organization of local and regional governments. In the U.S., many local governments have emergency management agencies that coordinate community resources in the event of disasters like tornadoes. This is especially true for major and moderately large cities. In the event that such coordinating agencies are absent at the local municipal level, nearly every county and state government have some type of emergency management arm of government that has the responsibility of disaster relief—this in addition to federal government agencies. Furthermore, there are a host of national charitable and nonprofit organizations that supplement relief efforts for areas and families affected by tornado-related disasters.[13]

Summary

Over the last half-century of studying and researching tornadoes, meteorologists and other scientists have learned more about these destructive storms—enough to develop technologies that detect them and warn communities that might be impacted by them. Because of this, deaths and injuries from twisters have—on the whole—been dramatically reduced. The National Weather Service and NOAA can often provide forecast alerts for conditions—sometimes days in advance—that may lead to the potential for severe weather and possible tornado outbreaks. However, planning ahead should not wait until the day of an expected outbreak or during the heart of the severe weather season.

Tornadoes can occur at any time of the year, and any time of the day. Erring on the side of over-preparation and assuming that the worst will happen when a tornado warning is issued is more preferable than not taking a tornado warning seriously and being caught unprepared. Many times, tornado warnings may result in no actual tornado touching down, resulting in time spent seemingly unnecessarily in a shelter. However, relatively speaking, tornado warnings over the years have become good enough that every one issued needs to be taken seriously.

Individuals and families should take the initiative and take responsibility for their safety. Plans for their individual should be made before a tornado or any predictable crisis. It is important to make decisions about the safest places to take shelter prior to their need. While statistically it is not likely that a tornado will strike a particular community, but being prepared for the possibility will ensure individual safety should it happen.

Advances in technology and years of scientific studies have improved our understanding of the ingredients and conditions needed to create a tornado. Thanks to this improved understanding, scientists are able to ascertain the best means—given the numerous individual factors for any given storm—people can best protect themselves from these vicious forces of nature. However, an ability to precisely predict when and where tornadoes will strike a given area is *still* lacking on some levels. The average *lead time*—the time period between the issuing of a tornado warning and its actual formation

---

[13] For a list of contact information for national, regional, state, and territorial government emergency management offices, see Appendixes A and B. Appendix C list provincial emergency management contact information for Canada. Appendix D lists the major charitable and non-profit disaster-relief contact organizations. Organizations in Appendix D would be (an) idea beginning point to secure assistance for needs such as assisting homeowners without insurance.

or appearance as a threat to a populated area—is only between 13 and 16 minutes. Although this doesn't sound like a lot of time to search for and secure shelter in the event of a tornado, it's an actual vast improvement of tornado lead time from the early 1990s, when lead time was approximately 5-10 minutes. But *any* available time used in preparation to ensure tornado safety, particularly during a period when tornadoes are a threat is time that is well-invested.

Points To Remember

- Although there is no absolute safe place from a tornado, the safest place to be statistically is in a basement (under a sturdy table or workbench) or a reinforced safe room.
- Weather radios, weather-related computer and cell phone applications, and local internet weather-related sites (including local news sites) are a good way to stay informed if during inclimate and/or threatening weather.
- **If weather conditions become threatening, and there is a lingering doubt that the current residence isn't suitable protection from a tornado, occupants should head to a building that stands a better chance of withstanding such a storm.** Head to a neighbor's or a local business. Ask if for permission to ride out the storm with them.
- In homes without basements and/or safe rooms, the best course of action is to plan ahead for where to take shelter in the event of a tornado. In such a dwelling, taking shelter in far interior rooms (with as many walls between the occupants and the outside of the structure) is the best course of action.
- Many businesses and other places of public accommodation (such as public schools and government offices) have procedures and protocols in place in the event of emergencies such as tornadoes. In addition, many of these same facilities have tend to have designated individuals in charge of coordinating and/or overseeing these procedures. It is advisable that in the event of a tornado to know these procedures or the personnel in charge of implementing them.
- If caught in a vehicle during an approaching tornado, it is not advisable to try to outrun a tornado. However, there are times when it might be necessary or possible to either attempt to outmaneuver a twister by driving in a direction away from its path, or to take other immediate and decisive action to avoid injury or death. The best way to attempt this is to drive at right angles of the approaching funnel, with one line segment repenting an unoccupied and the other representing the actual funnel of an approaching tornado (such as driving in the perpendicular path in the lines of a "T" formation, with one line segment representing the path of a tornado, and the intersecting line representing the suggested driving path). In this particular scenario, the options are very limited. They are: get out of the vehicle and take cover in a ditch, gully, or other type of low ground-level indentation, or to attempt to ride out the storm in a vehicle (which has no guarantee of being safe, but might not be an option under particular circumstances).

- In tornado-prone areas, planning ahead is *the* single best factor in limiting the potential for death or serious injury in the aftermath of a tornado. Monitoring weather advisories, planning where to take shelter, purchasing and storing emergencies supplies, and being confident in success planning are the best ways to increase the odds that a tornado emergency will have a relatively positive outcome. Know the contact information of your city, state, and federal emergency management offices (see: Appendixes A and B).

Notes

Tornado History

The following tornado-related events are notable for the particular extreme weather records they produced, as well as providing an illustration of the varying impact and effects these storms represent.

Date	Location	Impact/Significance
April 26, 1989	Daulatpur-Saturia, Bangladesh (Dhaka region)	The deadliest tornado on record, an estimated 1,300 people was killed by a twister that was estimated to have been 1 mile (1.6 km) wide, with a path between 25 – 50 miles (40-80 km). The Tri-State Tornado also holds the record for the fastest forward speed of a moving tornado at 73 mph (117 km/h) mph.
March 18, 1925	Southeastern Missouri, Southern Illinois, Southwestern Indiana	The "Tri-State Tornado" remains the deadliest tornado in U.S. history. The storm, which crossed over 3 different state regions, killed 695 people and injured more than 2,000.
May 31, 2013	El Reno, Union City, Oklahoma	An intense storm system striking the El Reno/Union City areas of Oklahoma spawned an EF-5 tornado that measured at one point 2.5 miles (4 km) wide, making it the widest tornado (funnel) ever recorded.
May 3, 1999	Bridge Creek/Moore City, Oklahoma	A portable Doppler radar unit measured the highest wind speeds ever recorded on earth within a mile wide tornado outside of Moore, Oklahoma. The recorded wind speeds reached 318 mph (511 Km/h).
April 25–28, 2011	Southern, Midwest, North-eastern United States, and Southern Canada	The largest tornado outbreak ever recorded occurred over a period of 3 days, the severe weather outbreak produced some 358 confirmed tornadoes, resulting in 324 direct tornado deaths over a large area of the U.S. and Southern Canada.

The Conditions & Where (Else) Around the Globe Tornadoes Occur

Glossary of Tornado-Related Terms

Bow echo- A bow-shaped radar signature associated with fast-moving storm systems accompanied by damaging winds.

Fujita Scale (Fujita-Pearson Scale)-is a scaled rating used rate the intensity of a tornado by examining the damage caused by the tornado after it has passed over a man-made structure. The scale was named after the pioneering tornado researcher, Dr. Theodore "Ted" Fujita.

Funnel Cloud-A rotating column of air of condensed water droplets that extends down from a cloud but does not touching the ground. When a funnel cloud actually reaches the ground, it becomes a tornado.

Lead Time-Refers to the amount of time between when a tornado warning is issued, and the actual formation (or sighting) of a tornado. Lead time is important in the ability to secure shelter in a reasonable amount of time during a tornado threat.

Mesocyclone-A column of strong spinning winds found within a supercell thunderstorm. These wind columns begin spinning horizontally (perpendicular to the ground), and then shift vertically (due to the presence of wind shear), sometimes forming becoming a tornado funnel.

Multiple Vortex Tornado-A tornado during which, more than one condensation funnel is present at the same time, and are rotating around the same common center. Multi-vortex tornadoes can be among the most violent. Similar to "satellite tornadoes."

Rope Tornado-A narrow funnel, or tornado that resembles a rope and is usually seen in the decaying states of a tornado.

Satellite Tornadoes-Smaller tornadoes that sometimes spin are off a "parent" (or main) tornado. Satellite tornadoes can develop and travel their own paths, creating an additional level of destruction during a supercell thunderstorm.

Squall Line-A line of thunderstorms, moving as one unit. Squall lines can move along a quickly advancing cold front. The main threats from a squall line are heavy rain, strong winds, hail. Tornadoes are also possible associated with bow echoes.

Supercells-Powerful types of thunderstorms that often give birth to mesocyclones and sometimes spawning tornadoes.

Tornado Alley-A geographic area located in the central portion of the U.S. that stretches from Northern Texas through Nebraska, east into Iowa and parts of extreme Southern Minnesota, north into the Dakotas. This area represents a zone where more tornadoes occur than any other region on the planet.

Tornado Watch-A severe weather alert issued when weather conditions in the given area are favorable for the formation of a tornado.

The No-Nonsense Guide To Tornado Safety

Tornado Warning-A severe weather alert issued when an actual tornado funnel has been sighted, or detected electronically by weather radar in or around your area.

Wall Cloud-A localized, and often rapid lowering cloud formation from the cloud base. Wall clouds form in the lower portion of a strong updraft, usually associated with a supercell. Normally found on the south or southwest wide of a thunderstorm, wall clouds that exhibit persistent, sustained rotation can often precede tornado formation.

Waterspout-A tornado that occurs over a large body of water, such as a lake or an ocean.

Wedge Tornado-A tornado that appears wider than it is tall, and has a wedge-like appearance. A tornado's destruction cannot be defined by its size, but some of the most violent tornadoes have been reported as a wedge.

Windshear- A change in wind speed or direction with height in the atmosphere. This often results in a rapid change in winds over a short horizontal distance, which is a primary factor in the formation of tornadoes.

Wind-tunnel Effect—The natural increase in the force and speed of winds that are forced through a narrow area. This phenomenon is the reason why taking shelter under a highway overpass during a tornado is not advised; those doing so could easily be swept out by the added force of already powerful tornado winds forced through such a confined area.

The No-Nonsense Guide To Tornado Safety

Appendix A:

Federal Emergency Management Agency (FEMA) contact information by region

As an extensive government agency, FEMA administrative resources (as well as contact information) have been somewhat decentralized. This is to say that, in order to expedite any assistance to local and state governments (and to limit the potential for bureaucratic confusion), FEMA was divided into regional offices that oversee regional "zones." These *Regional Operations Offices* serve as the arms of the central agency's headquarters (located in Washington D.C.) and through which all policy, managerial, resource and administrative actions effecting coordination between headquarters are initiated.

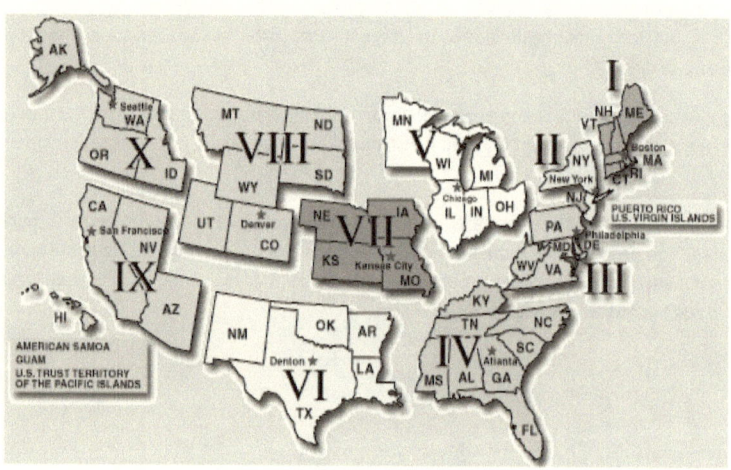

Region	Location	States Serving
Region I	Boston, MA	CT, MA, ME, NH, RI, VT
Region II	New York, NY	NJ, NY, PR, USVI
Region III	Philadelphia, PA	DC, DE, MD, PA, VA, WV
Region IV	Atlanta, GA	AL, FL, GA, KY, MS, NC, SC, TN
Region V	Chicago, IL	IL, IN, MI, MN, OH, WI
Region VI	Denton, TX	AR, LA, NM, OK, TX

The No-Nonsense Guide To Tornado Safety

Region	Location	States Serving
Region VII	Kansas City, MO	IA, KS, MO, NE
Region VIII	Denver, CO	CO, MT, ND, SD, UT, WY
Region IX	Oakland, CA	AZ, CA, HI, NV, GU, AS, CNMI, RMI, FM
Region X	Bothell, WA	AK, ID, OR, WA

Contact:

FEMA Region I
99 High St.
Boston, MA 02110
1-877-336-2734
Email

Federal Region II
26 Federal Plaza
New York, NY 10278-0002
Telephone: (212) 680-3600
FEMA-R2-ExternalAffairs@fema.dhs.gov

Puerto Rico and Virgin Islands

Mailing address:
Carribean Division
PO Box 70105
San Juan PR 00936-0105

Physical address:
New San Juan Office Bldg
159 Calle Chardon, 6th Floor
Hato Rey, PR 00918
Telephone: (787) 296-3500

FEMA Region III
One Independence Mall, 6th Floor
615 Chestnut Street
Philadelphia, PA 19106-4404
(215) 931-5500

FEMA Region IV
Federal Emergency Management Agency
3003 Chamblee Tucker Road
Atlanta, GA 30341

Office: 770-220-5200
Fax Number: 770-220-5230

FEMA Region V
Federal Emergency Management Agency
536 South Clark Street, 6th Floor
Chicago, IL 60605
(312) 408-5500

FEMA Region VI
Federal Emergency Management Agency
FRC 800 North Loop 288
Denton, TX 76209-3698
E-Mail: FEMA-R6-RRCC-PrivateSector@fema.dhs.gov
Tribal Affairs
E-Mail Norma.Reyes@fema.dhs.gov
Telephone: 940-898-5233

FEMA Region VII or Federal Emergency Management Agency
9221 Ward Parkway, Suite 300
Kansas City, MO. 64114-3372
Telephone: (816) 283-7061
Tribal Contact
E-mail: jonathan.weinberg@fema.dhs.gov
Telephone: (816) 809-4128

FEMA Region VIII or Federal Emergency Management Agency
Federal Emergency Management Agency
Denver Federal Center
Building 710, Box 25267
Denver, CO 80225-0267
(303) 235-4800

FEMA Region IX
1111 Broadway, Oakland, CA 94607
Phone:(510) 627-7140
Pacific Area Office
(808) 851-7900
Southern California Field Office
(626) 431-3000

FEMA Region X or Federal Emergency Management Agency
Federal Regional Center
130 - 228th Street, Southwest
Bothell, WA 98021-8627
(425) 487-4600

Appendix B:
State Offices and Agencies of Emergency Management
U.S.

A

Alabama Emergency Management Agency
5898 County Road 41
P.O. Drawer 2160
Clanton, Alabama 35046-2160
(205) 280-2476
(205) 280-2442 FAX
http://ema.alabama.gov/

Alaska Division of Homeland Security and Emergency Management
P.O. Box 5750
Fort Richardson, Alaska 99505-5750
(907) 428-7000
(907) 428-7009 FAX
http://www.ak-prepared.com/

American Samoa Territorial Emergency Management Coordination
(TEMCO)
American Samoa Government
P.O. Box 1086
Pago Pago, American Samoa 96799
(011)(684) 699-6415
(011)(684) 699-6414 FAX

Arizona Division of Emergency Management
5636 E. McDowell Road
Phoenix, Arizona 85008-3495
(800) 411-2336 | (602) 244-0504
(602) 464-6356 FAX
http://www.dem.azdema.gov/

Arkansas Department of Emergency Management
Bldg. # 9501
Camp Joseph T. Robinson
North Little Rock, Arkansas 72199-9600

The No-Nonsense Guide To Tornado Safety

(501) 683-6700
(501) 683-7890 FAX
www.adem.arkansas.gov/

C

California Emergency Management Agency
3650 Schriever Avenue
Mather, California 95655
(916) 845-8506
(916) 845-8511 FAX http://www.calema.ca.gov/Pages/default.aspx

Colorado Division Homeland Security and Emergency Management
Department of Public Safety
9195 E. Mineral Avenue
Suite 200
Centennial, Colorado 80112
(720) 852-6600
(720) 852-6750 Fax
http://www.dhsem.state.co.us/ or http://www.coemergency.com/

Connecticut Office of Emergency Management
Department of Emergency Management and Homeland Security
25 Sigourney Street 6th floor
Hartford, Connecticut 06106-5042
(860) 256-0800
(860) 256-0815 FAX
www.ct.gov/demhs/

D

Delaware Emergency Management Agency
165 Brick Store Landing Road
Smyrna, Delaware 19977
(302) 659-3362
(302) 659-6855 FAX
http://www.dema.delaware.gov/

District of Columbia Emergency Management Agency
2720 Martin Luther King, Jr. Avenue, S.E.
Second Floor
Washington, D.C. 20032
(202) 727-6161
(202) 673-2290 FAX
http://hsema.dc.gov/

F

Florida Division of Emergency Management

The No-Nonsense Guide To Tornado Safety

2555 Shumard Oak Blvd.
Tallahassee, Florida 32399-2100
(850) 413-9969
(850) 488-1016 FAX
http://www.floridadisaster.org/index.asp

G

Georgia Emergency Management Agency
935 East Confederate Ave SE
P.O. Box 18055
Atlanta, Georgia 30316-0055
(404) 635-7000
(404) 635-7205 FAX
http://www.gema.state.ga.us/

Guam Homeland Security/Office of Civil Defense
221B Chalan Palasyo
Agana Heights, Guam 96910
Tel:(671)475-9600
Fax:(671)477-3727
http://ghs.guam.gov/

H

Hawaii State Civil Defense
3949 Diamond Head Road
Honolulu, Hawaii 96816-4495
(808) 733-4300
(808) 733-4287 FAX
http://www.scd.hawaii.gov/

I

Idaho Bureau of Homeland Security
4040 Guard Street, Bldg. 600
Boise, Idaho 83705-5004
(208) 422-3040
(208) 422-3044 FAX
http://www.bhs.idaho.gov/

Illinois Emergency Management Agency
2200 S. Dirksen Pkwy.
Springfield, Illinois 62703
Office: (217) 782-2700 or (217) 782-2700
Fax: (217) 557-1978
http://www.state.il.us/iema/

Indiana Department of Homeland Security
Indiana Government Center South
302 West Washington Street, Room E208
Indianapolis, Indiana 46204-2767
Office: (317) 232-3986
Fax: (317) 232-3895
http://www.in.gov/dhs/emermgtngpgm.htm

Indiana State Emergency Management Agency
302 West Washington Street
Room E-208 A
Indianapolis, Indiana 46204-2767
(317) 232-3986
(317) 232-3895 FAX
http://www.in.gov/dhs/index.html

Iowa Homeland Security & Emergency Management Division
7105 NW 70th Ave, Camp Dodge
Building W-4
Johnston, Iowa 50131
(515) 725-3231
(515) 281-3260 FAX
http://www.iowahomelandsecurity.org/

K

Kansas Division of Emergency Management
2800 S.W. Topeka Boulevard
Topeka, Kansas 66611-1287
(785) 274-1409
(785) 274-1426 FAX
http://www.kansastag.gov/kdem_default.asp

Kentucky Emergency Management
EOC Building
100 Minuteman Parkway Bldg. 100
Frankfort, Kentucky 40601-6168
(502) 607-1682 or (800) 255-2587
(502) 607-1614 FAX
http://kyem.ky.gov/Pages/default.aspx

L

Louisiana Office of Emergency Preparedness
7667 Independence Blvd.
Baton Rouge, Louisiana 70806
(225) 925-7500

The No-Nonsense Guide To Tornado Safety

(225) 925-7501 FAX
http://www.gohsep.la.gov/

M

Maine Emergency Management Agency
#72 State House Station
45 Commerce Drive, Suite #2
Augusta, Maine 04333-0072
(207) 624-4400
(207) 287-3180 (FAX)
http://www.maine.gov/mema/

CNMI Emergency Management Office
Office of the Governor
Commonwealth of the Northern Mariana Islands
P.O. Box 10007
Saipan, Mariana Islands 96950
(670) 322-9529
(670) 322-7743 FAX
http://www.cnmiemo.gov.mp/

National Disaster Management Office
Office of the Chief Secretary
P.O. Box 15
Majuro, Republic of the Marshall Islands 96960-0015
(011)(692) 625-5181
(011)(692) 625-6896 FAX

Maryland Emergency Management Agency
Camp Fretterd Military Reservation
5401 Rue Saint Lo Drive
Reistertown, Maryland 21136
(410) 517-3600
(877) 636-2872 Toll-Free
(410) 517-3610 FAX
http://mema.maryland.gov/Pages/homePreparedness_heat.aspx

Massachusetts Emergency Management Agency
400 Worcester Road
Framingham, Massachusetts 01702-5399
(508) 820-2000
(508) 820-2030 FAX
http://www.mass.gov/eopss/agencies/mema/

Michigan State Police, Emergency Management & Homeland Security Division
Michigan Dept. of State Police
4000 Collins Road

Lansing, Michigan 48909-8136
(517) 333-5042
(517) 333-4987 FAX
http://www.michigan.gov/msp/0,1607,7-123-1593_3507---,00.html

National Disaster Control Officer
Federated States of Micronesia
P.O. Box PS-53
Kolonia, Pohnpei - Micronesia 96941
(011)(691) 320-8815
(001)(691) 320-2785 FAX

Minnesota Homeland Security and Emergency Management Division
Minnesota Dept. of Public Safety
444 Cedar Street, Suite 223
St. Paul, MN 55101-6223
Office: (651) 201-7400
Fax: (651) 296-0459
https://dps.mn.gov/divisions/hsem/Pages/default.aspx

Mississippi Emergency Management Agency
P.O. Box 5644
Pearl, MS 39288-5644
(601) 933-6362
(800) 519-6362 Toll Free
(601) 933-6800 FAX
http://www.msema.org/

Missouri Emergency Management Agency
2302 Militia Drive
P.O. Box 116
Jefferson City, Missouri 65102
(573) 526-9100
(573) 634-7966 FAX
http://sema.dps.mo.gov/

JFHQ-MT
Montana Division of Disaster & Emergency Services
1956 Mt Majo Street
PO BOX 4789
Fort Harrison, Montana 59636-4789
(406) 841-3911
(406) 841-3965 FAX

http://www.dma.mt.gov/des/

N

Nebraska Emergency Management Agency
1300 Military Road

Lincoln, Nebraska 68508-1090
(402) 471-7421
(402) 471-7433 FAX
http://www.nema.ne.gov/index.shtml

Nevada Division of Emergency Management
2478 Fairview Dr
Carson City, Nevada 89701
(775) 687-0300
(775) 687-0330FAX
http://dem.nv.gov/

Governor's Office of Emergency Management
State Office Park South
33 Hazen Dr
Concord, New Hampshire 03305
(603) 271-2231
(603) 271-3609 FAX
http://www.nh.gov/safety/divisions/hsem/

New Jersey State Police
New Jersey Office of Emergency Management
P.O. Box 7068, River RD
West Trenton, New Jersey 08628-0068
(609) 882-2000 ext 2700 Monday to Friday
(609) 963-6900 Emergency
(609) 963-6208 Mitigation
(609) 963-6992 State Training Officer
(609) 671-0160 Fax
http://www.ready.nj.gov/

New Mexico Department of Homeland Security
and Emergency Management (DHSEM)
13 Bataan Boulevard
P.O. Box 27111
Santa Fe, New Mexico 87502
(505) 476-9600
(505) 476-9635 Emergency
(505) 476-9695 FAX
http://www.nmdhsem.org/

New York State Emergency Management Office
1220 Washington Avenue
Building 22, Suite 101
Albany, New York 12226-2251
(518) 292-2275
(518) 322-4978 FAX
http://www.dhses.ny.gov/oem/

North Carolina Division of Emergency Management - Main Office

The No-Nonsense Guide To Tornado Safety

1636 Gold Star Drive
4236 Mail Service Center
Raleigh, N.C. 27607-3371
(919) 825-2500
Emergency Management 24-Hour Operations 1-800-858-0368
https://www.ncdps.gov/Index2.cfm?a=000003,000010

North Dakota Department of Emergency Services
P.O. Box 5511
Bismarck, North Dakota 58506-5511
(701) 328-8100
(701) 328-8181 FAX
http://www.nd.gov/des/

O

Ohio Emergency Management Agency
2855 West Dublin-Granville Road
Columbus, Ohio 43235-2206
Office: (614) 889-7150
Fax: (614) 889-7183
http://ema.ohio.gov/

Oklahoma Department of Emergency Management
2401 Lincoln Blvd Suite C51
Oklahoma City, Oklahoma 73105
(405) 521-2481
(405) 521-4053 FAX
http://www.ok.gov/OEM/

Oregon Emergency Management
Department of State Police
3225 State St
Salem, Oregon 97309-5062
(503) 378-2911
(503) 373-7833 FAX
http://www.oregon.gov/OMD/OEM/Pages/index.aspx

P

Palau NEMO Coordinator
Office of the President
P.O. Box 100
Koror, Republic of Palau 96940
(011)(680) 488-2422
(011)(680) 488-3312

Pennsylvania Emergency Management Agency
2605 Interstate Drive
Harrisburg PA 17110-9463

The No-Nonsense Guide To Tornado Safety

(717) 651-2001
(717) 651-2040 FAX
http://www.pema.state.pa.us/portal/server.pt/community/pema_home/4463

Puerto Rico Emergency Management Agency
P.O. Box 966597
San Juan, Puerto Rico 00906-6597
(787) 724-0124
(787) 725-4244 FAX
http://www2.pr.gov/Directorios/Pages/InfoAgencia.aspx?PRIFA=021

R

Rhode Island Emergency Management Agency
645 New London Ave
Cranston, Rhode Island 02920-3003
(401) 946-9996
(401) 944-1891 FAX
http://www.riema.ri.gov/

S

South Carolina Emergency Management Division
2779 Fish Hatchery Road
West Columbia South Carolina 29172
(803) 737-8500
(803) 737-8570 FAX
http://www.scemd.org/

South Dakota Division of Emergency Management
118 West Capitol
Pierre, South Dakota 57501
(605) 773-3231
(605) 773-3580 FAX
http://dps.sd.gov/emergency_services/emergency_management/

T

Tennessee Emergency Management Agency
3041 Sidco Drive
Nashville, Tennessee 37204-1502
(615) 741-0001
(615) 242-9635 FAX
http://www.tnema.org/

Texas Division of Emergency Management
5805 N. Lamar
PO BOX 4087
Austin, Texas 78773-0220

The No-Nonsense Guide To Tornado Safety

(512) 424-2138
(512) 424-2444 or 7160 FAX
http://www.txdps.state.tx.us/dem/

U

Utah Division of Emergency Services and Homeland Security
1110 State Office Building
P.O. Box 141710
Salt Lake City, Utah 84114-1710
(801) 538-3400
(801) 538-3770 FAX
http://publicsafety.utah.gov/emergencymanagement/

V

Vermont Emergency Management Agency
Department of Public Safety
Waterbury State Complex
103 South Main Street
Waterbury, Vermont 05671-2101
(802) 244-8721
(800) 347-0488
(802) 244-8655 FAX
http://dps.vermont.gov/

Virgin Islands Territorial Emergency Management - VITEMA
2-C Contant, A-Q Building
Virgin Islands 00820
(340) 774-2244
(340) 774-1491

Virginia Department of Emergency Management
10501 Trade Court
Richmond, VA 23236-3713
(804) 897-6500
(804) 897-6556 FAX
http://www.vaemergency.gov/

W

State of Washington Emergency Management Division
Building 20, M/S: TA-20
Camp Murray, Washington 98430-5122
(253) 512-7000
(800) 562-6108
(253) 512-7200 FAX
http://www.emd.wa.gov/

The No-Nonsense Guide To Tornado Safety

West Virginia Office of Emergency Services
Building 1, Room EB-80 1900 Kanawha Boulevard, East
Charleston, West Virginia 25305-0360
(304) 558-5380
(304) 344-4538 FAX
http://www.dhsem.wv.gov/Pages/default.aspx
Wisconsin Emergency Management
2400 Wright Street
P.O. Box 7865
Madison, Wisconsin 53707-7865
Phone: (608) 242-3232
Fax: (608) 242-3247
http://emergencymanagement.wi.gov/

Wyoming Homeland Security Training Program
1556 Riverbend Drive
Douglas WY 82633
(307) 358-1920
(307) 358-0994 FAX
http://wyohomelandsecurity.state.wy.us/

Appendix C:
Provincial Offices and Agencies of Emergency Management
Canada

The following list comprises the provincial and territorial emergency management organizations (EMOs) for Canada. These EMOs are responsible for granting administrative, logistical support and assistance, as well as other needed resources to local governments in times of emergencies such as tornadoes.

Alberta
Alberta Emergency Management Agency
Telephone: (780) 422-9000 / Toll-free: 310-0000
www.aema.alberta.ca

British Columbia
British Columbia Provincial Emergency Program
Telephone: (250) 952-4913 / Emergency: 1-800-663-3456
www.pep.bc.ca

Manitoba
Manitoba Emergency Measures Organization
Telephone: (204) 945-4772 / Toll-free: 1-888-267-8298
www.manitobaemo.ca

New Brunswick
New Brunswick Emergency Measures Organization
Telephone: (506) 453-2133 / Toll-free 24 Hour line: 1-800-561-4034
www.gnb.ca/cnb/emo-omu

Newfoundland and Labrador
Newfoundland and Labrador Fire and Emergency Services
Telephone: (709) 729-3703
www.ma.gov.nl.ca/ma/fes

Northwest Territories
Northwest Territories Emergency Management Organization
Telephone: (867) 873-7538 / 24 Hour line: (867) 920-2303
www.maca.gov.nt.ca/emergency_management/index.htm

Nova Scotia
Nova Scotia Emergency Management Office

The No-Nonsense Guide To Tornado Safety

Telephone Toll-free 24 Hour line: 1-866-424-5620
www.gov.ns.ca/emo

Nunavut
Nunavut Emergency Management
Telephone: (867) 975-5403 / Toll-free 24 Hour line: 1-800-693-1666
http://cgs.gov.nu.ca/en/commEmergency.aspx

Ontario
Emergency Management Ontario
Telephone: (416) 314-3723 / Toll-free 24 Hour line: 1-877-314-3723
www.ontario.ca/emo

Prince Edward Island
Prince Edward Island Emergency Measures Organization
Telephone: (902) 894-0385 / After hours: (902) 892-9365
www.peipublicsafety.ca

Quebec
Quebec – Ministère de la sécurité publique
Telephone (toll-free): 1-866-644-6826
General information (Services Québec): 1-877-644-4545
www.securitepublique.gouv.qc.ca

Saskatchewan
Saskatchewan Emergency Management Organization
Telephone: (306) 787-9563
www.gr.gov.sk.ca/SaskEMO

Yukon
Yukon Emergency Measures Organization
Telephone: (867) 667-5220
Toll free (within the Yukon): 1-800-661-0408
www.community.gov.yk.ca/emo

Appendix D:

Disaster-Relief Organizations and Charities

This following is a partial list of the many disaster-relief and charitable organizations that those affected by tornado emergencies can turn to in times of need. Below is a sample of the most notable of these organizations.

American Red Cross
http://www.redcross.org/find-help

Catholic Charities USA
http://www.catholiccharitiesusa.org/what-we-do/disaster-operations/

Children's Disaster Services (Church of the Brethren)
http://www.brethren.org/cds/

Christian Disaster Response
http://cdresponse.org/

Feeding America
http://feedingamerica.org/need-help.aspx?s_src=Y14YPDGAA&s_keyword=feedingamerica&s_subsrc=feedingamerica

National Organization for Victim Assistance (NOVA)
http://www.trynova.org/

Salvation Army
http://www.salvationarmyusa.org/

Jewish federations of North America
http://www.jewishfederations.org/

World Vision
http://www.worldvision.org/m/sponsor-a-child/?open&campaign=1193512&cmp=KNC-1193512&gclid=CI-G67v8pboCFYSd4AodMhgAIA

Appendix E:
Useful Smart Phones & Computer App (Applications)

1.   <u>Red Cross – Tornado</u> (Free)

The American Red Cross-sponsored Tornado App is an interactive program downloadable to most smart phones. It contains an interactive quiz related to tornado safety, as well as advice in the event of a tornado. This app also has an audible siren when NOAA issues a Tornado warning for any of your monitored locations (Note: Alerts' sounds will NOT override if phone is on vibrate or in sleep mode).

2.   <u>Tornado Alert</u> (Free)

Created and sponsored by WraithNet, this app utilizes a network of other users to inform each other of an imminent tornado threat for a particular alert area (within 20 miles). Alerts are normally delivered to all users in less than 5 seconds. In addition to this, users are notified whenever either a a "Tornado Watch" or "Tornado Warning" is issued for an area, within 1 minute of the alert being declared.

3.   <u>Weather Bug</u> (Free)

An all-around weather app for both phones and computers (<u>Weather Bug Desktop</u>), Weather Bug provides real-time weather forecasts for the users' vicinity for a 10-day period. In addition, this app contains a real-time sensor that warns of dangerous lightning threats for the users' area. Created and sponsored by Earth Networks.

4.   <u>The Weather Channel</u> (Free)

Also available for <u>desktop/laptop</u> computers , this app—like Weather Bug—provides an active 10-day weather forecast for the user vicinity. In addition, the issues real-time severe weather bulletins such as those issued for tornadoes.

Many other similar applications of various costs can be found by searching various online application sources such as Google Play and the Apple-supported i-Tunes .

Appendix E:

Local Public Tornado Shelters

The following are a list of established and designated tornado shelters as listed from various news sources and social networking sites. The list is composed of those shelters established by local municipalities (i.e., city government-designated or owned) as well as privately owned and operated shelters (e.g., those operated by civil organizations, churches, and/or private citizens who have made their facilities available to those in need in times of a tornado emergency). The list is as accurate and up-to-date as changing economic policies and resources will allow (i.e., some local municipalities have opted to close their public tornado shelters due to budgetary or liability concerns). It is advisable to contact these facilities and/or their respective operators to ascertain whether shelters are still available for use in the event of a tornado emergency. Also, consider the dangers of attempting to travel to locate a public tornado shelter in the event of a tornado warning. Although the average lead time for a tornado is between 13-16 minutes, some tornadoes give far less time to reach a shelter. Generally, FEMA suggest that shelters should be considered a primary option *if* it is possible to reach one within 5 minutes of an issued tornado warning, otherwise it is advisable to seek shelter around one's current location. All shelters will likely have limited space, so being aware of threatening weather conditions is key to considering their use as an option.

Alabama

Anderson:
First Baptist Church of Anderson-245 Church St.
Goodsprings Community Shelter-33634 AL Hwy. 99 (holds 150 people).

Albertville:
Albertville Board of Education
107 West Main Street

Arab:
Arab Senior Center-800 North Main Street
Mount Oak United Methodist Church-3384 Ruth Road

Attalla:
Stowers Hill Baptist Church-407 Ninth Ave. SW

Athens:
Pleasant Grove Safe Room
9080 Upper Snake Road
Holds 150 people
Owens Elementary School-21465 AL Hwy. 99 (holds 600 people). Will be open to the public after school hours only

Belgreen:
Shelter Near Belgreen School Gym
14141 Hwy 187

Burnout:
Burnout Fire Department-75 Hwy 224

The No-Nonsense Guide To Tornado Safety

Cherokee:
1211 2nd Street

Columbiana:
Behind the Southeast Shelby Rescue Building

Courtland:
Roy Coffee Park
3581 Jefferson Street

Cullman:
Cullman County Courthouse Basement (opens when tornado watch issued)
Vinemont/Providence Fire Stations #1 & #2 (each will hold 100 people)

Crossville:
Fire Department (holds 96 people).

Danville:
6619 County Road 81 Danville Volunteer Fire Department-5798 Hwy 36 West (2 shelters at this location – both hold 98 people).
Massey Volunteer Fire Department-386 Evergreen Road (holds 98 people).
Punkin Center Volunteer Fire Department-116 Kirby Bridge Road (holds 98 people).

Decatur:
Decatur City Hall (Basement)
Morgan County EMA (first floor of Morgan County Courthouse) 302 Lee Street NE

Elgin:
Elgin United Methodist Church
2743 Hwy 101

Florence:
North Wood United Methodist Church-1129 N Wood Ave
Petersville Church of Christ-3601 Cloverdale Rd.
Underwood/Petersville Community Center-840 County Road 7
Stoney Point Church of Christ-1755 County Road 24

Ford City:
14439 County Line Road

Fort Payne:
DeKalb County Activities Building (basement – can hold about 200 people)

Fyffe: Senior Center-413 Graves Street (holds about 20 people)
Fyffe Town Hall (holds 96 people).
Fyffe Church of God-778 Main Street (please call first to see if shelter is open).

Gadsden:
Etowah Baptist Association-853 Walnut St.
Gadsden Public Library-254 College St.
Goodyear Heights Baptist Church-608 Kaying Rd. N
NE Etowah Community Center-3733 US Hwy 411 N
Paden Baptist Church-900 Padenreich Ave

Garden City:
Town Hall
501 1st Avenue S
(will hold 500 people)

The No-Nonsense Guide To Tornado Safety

Geraldine:
Town Hall

Grant:
Grant Community Shelter-21 1st Avenue West
Hebron Community Shelter-90 Hebron School Road
Mt. Pleasant Community Shelter-5743 Simpson Point Road

Hanceville:
Dodge City Town Hall Basement (built to storm shelter standards)
202 Bangor Avenue SE
1407 Commercial Street SE
203 Michelle Street NW

Hodges:
Shelter (behind Hodges City Hall).-1842 Hwy. 172

Hokes Bluff/Piedmont:
Young's Chapel Methodist Church-44 Youngs Chapel Rd

Killen:
Killen United Methodist Church-201 J.C. Mauldin Hwy

Langston:
Langston Safe Room-9277 County Rd. 67
Wakefield Community Shelter-777 South Sauty Road

Leighton:
8856 Main Street

Lester:
Lester Community Shelter-30306 Lester Rd

Lexington:
Colonial Bank-11250 Hwy. 101
Mount Pleasant Baptist Church-8880 County Road 71
Lexington Town Hall-10914 Hwy. 101

Littleville:
1448 Jackson Highway
Madison:
Good Shepherd United Methodist Church-1418 Old Railroad Bed Rd

Madison:
Good Shepherd United Methodist Church-1418 Old Railroad Bed Road (this is not a county-run shelter; please call church first to see if it is open).

Moulton:
14201 Court Street

Mount Hope:
Mount Hope Senior Center-3142 County Road 460

Phil Campbell:
Phil Campbell Community Center-132 Sherry Bryce Dr.

Pleasant Site:
Pleasant Site Fire Department-2785 Hwy. 90

The No-Nonsense Guide To Tornado Safety

Priceville:
Priceville Town Hall (Basement)

Rainsville:
Plainview School (shelter can hold 600-700 people).

Red Bay:
Red Bay Water Park-640 2nd St NE
Red Bay Old Airport-627 9th Ave NW

Rogersville:
Rogersville United Methodist Church-51 Turner Lindsey Drive
Rogersville Church of Christ-450 College Street
First Baptist Church of Rogersville-222 College Street

Russellville:
Russellville Park & Rec Center-204 Ash Ave
511 Gaines Ave

Scottsboro:
Jackson County Courthouse (basement)-123 East Laurel Street (holds about 100 people).
Swearengin Community Shelter-5120 Swearengin Road,

Section:
Section City Hall-72 Dutton Rd

Shiloh:
Fire Department (holds 96 people).

Town Creek:
Red Bank Park-1933 County Road 314

Trinity:
Veterans Memorial Park-6229 County Road 214

Tuscumbia:
Colbert County EMA Office-120 West 5th Street

Union City:
Union Grove Community Shelter-3680 Union Grove Road
Union Grove Post Office Basement-3935 Union Grove Road,

Vina:
Vina Fire Department-79 Church Street

Waterloo:
Williams Chapel Presbyterian Church

Arkansas

Fort Smith:
In Fort Smith, the shelters are located at the elementary schools (Barling, Beard, Bonneville, Carnall, Cavanaugh, Cook, Euper lane, Fairview, Howard, Morrison, Orr, Pike, Spradling, Sunnymede, Sutton, Tilles, Trusty, and Woods). The shelters will open whenever tornado sirens are sounded..

River Valley/Alma:
Alma High School

The No-Nonsense Guide To Tornado Safety

Van Buren:
Rena Elementary-720 Rena Road
Van Buren High School-2001 Pointer Trail
Parkview Elementary-605 Parkview Street
Butterfield Trail Middle School-310 North 11th Street
King Elementary-401 North 19th Street
Tate Elementary-406 Catcher Road
Coleman Freshman Academy-821 East Pointer Trail
Note: Each shelter has been built to withstand wind speeds of up to 250mph and impact from flying debris. According to the NOAA (National Oceanic & Atmospheric Administration) EF4 tornados have wind speeds of 166-200mph while EF5 tornados have wind speeds in excess of 200mph. Butterfield Junior High and Van Buren High School shelters have a maximum capacity of 700 people. Parkview, Rena, Tate and King shelters have a maximum capacity of 500 people.

Colorado

Ellicott:
Ellicott High School Auditorium Community Shelter-375 S. Ellicott Hwy

Georgia:

Cordele:
Crisp County Sheriff's Department-196 Georgia 300 (community shelter on the southeast side of the Sheriff's Department).

Iowa:

Clear Lake:
Clear Lake State Park (for campers)
Veterans of Foreign Wars Post - Third and Main

Des Moines:
Iowa State Fairgrounds (dedicated storm shelter for 400 campers).

Mason City:
MacNider Campground

Nevada:
Nevada Public Library (a designated Tornado Shelter. The tornado shelter will be opened by the Nevada Police Department during tornado warnings).

Ventura:
Ventura Community Center-4 North Weimer Street (n the event of a weather emergency, the storm sirens are activated by police dispatch, the sirens transmit a signal to the Community Center to open the doors and activate a strobe light).

West Branch:
United Methodist Church-203 N. Downey St.

Kansas:

There is a semi-extensive network of storm shelters along the Kansas Turnpike, located primarily at toll plazas. These shelters were designed to provide a safe place for Kansas Turnpike Authority employees during severe weather, but depending on available space, travelers and members of the public may opt to take shelter in these areas. The following is a list of shelters along the Turnpike, along with their milepost/mile marker location, and location within the facility.

Shelter	Milepost/Mile marker	Location Within Facility
Southern Terminal	16.5	Basement of Toll Building

The No-Nonsense Guide To Tornado Safety

Wellington	19	Underground, West of Tollbooth
Belle Plaine Service Area	26	Convenience Store Storage Room
Mulvane (K-53)	33	Underground, West of Tollbooth
Mulvane (Casino)	33	Not Available
Haysville Derby	39	Underground, East of Tollbooth
South Wichita	42	Underground, West of Tollbooth
K-15	45	Underground, West of Tollbooth
East Wichita	50	Basement of Toll Office
K-96	53	Underground, East of Tollbooth
Andover	57	Underground, East of Tollbooth
Towanda Service Area	65	Large Restrooms
El Dorado	71	Underground, South of Tollbooth
North El Dorado	76	Underground, South of Tollbooth
Cassoday	92	Underground, Northeast of Tollbooth
Matfield Green Service Area	96	Large Restrooms
Emporia	127	Basement of Toll Building
Emporia Service Area	131	Convenience Store Restrooms
Admire	147	Underground, North of Tollbooth
South Topeka	183	Basement
Plaza 182 Exit	182	Underground, South of Tollbooth
East Topeka	183	Basement of Toll Building
Topeka Service Area	189	Basement
North Lecompton	197	Underground, South of Tollbooth
South Lecompton	197	Underground, North of Tollbooth
West Lawrence	202	Basement of Toll Building
East Lawrence	204	Not Available
Lawrence Service Area	209	Convenience Store Storage Room
Tonganoxie/Eudora	212	Not Available
Eastern terminal	217	Basement of Toll Building

In addition to those along the Kansas Turnpike, other public tornado shelters include (communities that offer safe rooms and/or basements for use as public tornado shelter unlocked these shelters during tornado warnings, even in the middle of the night):

Altamont:
Methodist Church, Basement (Haury Hall at the high school)

Andover:
Police department- 909 Andover Road
The Andover Public Library (equipped with tornado safe room).
Andover City Hall (equipped with tornado safe room).

Augusta:
Public Safety Building (Safe Room)-2100 N. Ohio

Baxter Springs:
Assembly of God Church-1245 Park Avenue

Bronson:
Cheney Witt Funeral- Hwy 54

Carterville:
First Baptist Church-200 E. Main
Chanute:
NCCC-800 W. 14th Street
NMRMC Hospital-629 S. Plummer
First Christian Church-102 North Grant

The No-Nonsense Guide To Tornado Safety

Otterbein Methodist-631 West 7th Street
First United Methodist-202 South Lincoln
St. Patrick's Catholic Church-424 South Central
Tioga Hotel, Basement-12 East Main Street
Fire Department, Memorial Building-8 East 2nd Street

Cheney:
Senior Center-516 N. Main

Cherryvale:
Public Library
United Methodist Church- 305 W 3rd S

Chetopa:
United Methodist Church- 305 W 3rd St
Coffeyville:
City Hall-7th & Walnut
Coffeyville Regional Medical Center
Community Elementary School (enter south Multi-Purpose Room door).
Fire Department -7th & Walnut
First Assembly of God Church-1504 W. 8th
First Church of God-5th & Cline
St. Paul's Lutheran Church-506 W. 9th St.

Columbus:
Park School Elementary
Cherokee County Court House-110 West Maple

Derby:
Fire Station No. 2-1401 N. Rock Road
Pleasant View Baptist Church-1335 N. Buckner

Douglass:
The Middle School's Support Facility-914 E. First St.

El Dorado:
City Hall Basement-220 E. 1st
Senior center-210 E. 2nd

Haysville :
City Hall-200 W. Grand

Park City:
City Hall- 6110 N. Hydraulic

Maize:
Community center, 401 S. Khedive
City Hall, 10100 Grady Ave. (use storm shelter entrance on front of building by flag pole)

Mulvane:
City Hall-211 N. 2nd (enter through the police department door on the east side)
EMS Station-910 E. Main

Rose Hill:
Christian Church-314 N. Rose Hill Road
First Baptist Church-1206 N. Rose Hill Road
Bible Church-1410 N. Main
United Methodist Youth Center-109 N. Main (use south door on Showalter)

The No-Nonsense Guide To Tornado Safety

City Hall, 125 W. Rosewood
Butler County Fire Station-911 N. Rose Hill Road

Valley Center:
Methodist Church-560 N. Park (has handicap lift)
Life Point Assembly of God-400 S. Abilene
Grace Connections-300 N. Ash (has single handicap chair lift)
Community Building-316 E. Clay

Wellington :
Sumner Regional Medical Center-1323 N. A St. (use southeast basement entrance; accepts pets in carriers)
Sumner Care Center-1600 W. 8th St. (use rear entrance under carport)
Old Junior High School-311 North A St. (use east entrance)

Mississippi

Amory:
West Amory Community Center- 111th Street
East Amory Community Center, Crump Boulevard
Amory Baseball Complex, Concord Avenue
Basement of City Hall, Front Street

Bruce:
Bruce Police/Fire Department (behind the station)-East Calhoun Street
Jimmy Beckley Drive- off Hwy 9 North/South Pontotoc Street

Blue Mountain:
Next to Blue Mountain Fire Dept-109 West Main St.

Carter's Branch:
Next to Fire Dept.

Coffeeville:
Skunna Valley Volunteer Fire Department-176 County Road 430
Clear Springs Volunteer Fire Department-1617 County Road 186

Dumas:
Behind Dumas Fire Dept-3340 Hwy 370

Houlka:
Houlka Fire Department-205 West Front Street

Houston:
Thorn Community Center-106 County Road 37
Rhodes Chapel Fire Department-1324 County Road 416
Pearsall Voting Precinct-105 County Road 91
Southeast Fire Department-1951 County Road 406
Houston Civic Center-635 Starkville Road
Houston Community Center-115 Dulaney Street
Houston Fire/Police Department-215 East Harrington Street
Houston Airport-601 Airport Road

Lafayette County

LCFD 9
65 County Road 335, Taylor

LCFD 15

The No-Nonsense Guide To Tornado Safety

4 County Road 109, (Hwy. 6 West of Oxford)

LCFD Central
50 County Road 1032, (Across from North Pointe)

Gordon Community Center
37 County Road 115, (South of Abbeville)

LCFD 7 (2 sets)
44 Business 7 South, (Abbeville)

Taylor Community Center
78 County Road 338, (Taylor)

New El Bethel Church
20 County Road 488, (Near Tula)

LCFD 1
599 Hwy. 310 (Harmontown)

LCFD 3
22 County Road 369, (Old Airport area near Hwy. 7 and 9W)

LCFD 4
8 County Road 130, (College Hill)

LCFD 5
826 Hwy. 334, (Yocona)

LCFD 6
153 County Road 436, (Tula)

LCFD 11
11 County Road 287, (Lafayette Springs)

LCFD 12
1301 Hwy. 30 East (Philadelphia)

LCFD 14
31 County Road 430 (Paris)

LCFD 16
823 County Road 313 (Union West)

Louisville:
County Courthouse (The basement of the courthouse is used during severe weather and open to the public).

Midway:
Midway Community Fire Station

Nettleton:
Nettleton Ball Park, 448 Union Avenue
Water Dept., 113 Johnson Drive
Near Nettleton Fire Department, Will Robins Hwy

Okolona:
Chickasaw County Admin Building (old jail site),-110 Olive Street
Okolona Police/Fire Department,-106 East Main Street

The No-Nonsense Guide To Tornado Safety

Okolona Public Works Building- 300 South Silver Street
Okolona City Hall- 215 East Main Street
Okolona National Guard Armory-214 West Monroe
Egypt Voting Precinct-253 County Road 177

Paden:
Next to Fire Dept.

Pittsboro:
Next to the Pittsboro Fire Department-East Main Street

Plantersville:
Plantersville Town Hall- 2587 Main Street

Pontotoc County:
There are 30 or more of the community tornado shelters are located in and around Pontotoc County. Typically, the shelters are located in, behind, or adjacent to municipal buildings such as fire and police departments, and emergency operations centers

Richmond:
Behind Richmond Volunteer Fire Dept-117 County Road 800

Ripley:
109 School Street
1005 City Ave North (hospital)
American Legion (Twin Lakes Road)
160 Bails Road
832 Ashland Road

Saltillo:
Birmingham Ridge Fire Dept-947 County Road 1948

Shannon:
Richardson Hill-31819 County Line Road

Tillatoba:
Tillatoba Volunteer Fire Department-27263 HWY 330

Tishomingo:
Tishomingo Fire Station

Tupelo:
843 North Front Street
Haven Community Center- 3288 Willie Moore Road

Van Vleet:
Chickasaw County Admin Building (old school location)-146 County Road 412

Water Valley:
O' Tuckolofa Volunteer Fire Department-55 County Road 118
Sylva Rena Volunteer Fire Department-187 County Road 57
Velma Volunteer Fire Department-12270 HWY 7
Pine Valley Volunteer Fire Department.-4454 HWY 32

Woodland:
Woodland Fire Department-101 Market Street
Anchor Voting Precinct-628 County Road 416
Atlanta Fire Department-1158 Highway 341 South
Sparta Opry House-762 County Road 419

The No-Nonsense Guide To Tornado Safety

Missouri

Ash Grove:
First Baptist Church-324 E Walker St.

Aurora:
Fire Department
City Hall Basement
Fire Station
Old Armory
First Baptist Church-201 S Jefferson Ave
First Christian Church-39 W Pleasant St,

Battlefield:
Baptist Church-5010 State Highway FF
United Methodist Church-5475 Daniel St.

Billings:
First Baptist Church-407 NE Pine St,
St. Joseph Catholic Church-320 NW Washington Ave.

Clever:
City Hall
First Baptist Church-105 Kennedy Ave

Eldon:
First Church of the Nazarene -1024 E Lawson Ave

Fair Grove:
United Methodist Church- 83 E Hickory
First Baptist Church-14 E Maple St,

Fordland:
Freewill Baptist Church- 266 S. Maple S
United Methodist Church-266 Maple St

Gainesville:
Ozark County Courthouse

Galena:
Law Enforcement Building (temporary facility)

Greentop:
Greentop Bapatist Church-202 E 1st S

Lebanon:
Police station in City Hall

Marionville:
First Baptist Church-301 S College Ave
First United Methodist Church- 117 S College Ave

Marshfield:
High School
Webster County Courthouse

Milan:

The No-Nonsense Guide To Tornado Safety

Sullivan County Courthouse

Miller:
American Legion Basement- 302 E Main St.

Pierce City:
City High School
Clark Community Health Center
National Guard Armory (holds about 75 people).
Downtown Fire Station

Poplar Bluff:
O'Neal Elementary School (Storm Shelter adjacent to school)

Republic:
Meadowview Baptist Church-Missouri 174 West at Kansas Avenue
Hope Lutheran Church-Missouri 174 at Hampton Avenue
Republic Nazarene Church-Lynn Avenue at Harrison Street

Stockton:
County Courthouse

West Plains:
Middle School-730 E. Olden St. (tornado-resistant safe room doubles as the school's gymnasium constructed to FEMA Standards).

Waynesville:
First Baptist Church (basement is opened up during tornado threats).

Webb City:
Public Library -101 South Liberty St. (When tornado sirens are sounded, an officer with the Webb City Police Department will open the Webb City Public Library as an emergency storm shelter. An officer will remain at the shelter until the severe weather threat has passed).

Willard:
New Life Baptist Church-414 E. New Melville Road
Willard Community Christian Church-300 E. Proctor

Nebraska

Columbus:
Platte County Courthouse Community Room (during business hours).

Ohio

McGuffey:
McGuffey Community Centre in Ohio

Oklahoma

Bethany:
Earl Harris Elementary - 4311 N. Asbury
Deaconess at Bethany - 7600 NW 23rd

The No-Nonsense Guide To Tornado Safety

Broken Arrow:
Johanna Woods Mobile Home Park-2909 E Montpelier St. (three shelters are designed to hold up to 170 community residents in each).

Del City:
City Hall, 371 S.E. 15th Street)

Forest Park:
Fire Station, 4203 N. Coltrane Road

Midwest City:
Reed Center - 5800 Will Rogers (off I-40 and Sooner Rd)
City Hall - 100 N. Midwest Blvd.
Fire Station #5 - 801 S. Westminster

Norman:
Irving Recreation Center - 1920 E. Alameda
Whittier Recreation Center - 2000 W. Brooks
Cleveland Elementary School - 500 N. Sherry
Little Axe High School - 168th Avenue N.E.
Note: The City of Norman doesn't own or operate any storm shelters that have been built to survive strong winds. In such an eventuality, the home is likely to be as safe as any other building in Norman (especially given the reality of the city's location within "Tornado Alley").

Shawnee:
Shawnee City Hall - 16 W. Ninth
Shawnee Fire Station No. 3 - 306 E. MacArthur St.

Stillwater
Public shelters located on the Oklahoma State University campus
Designated Buildings:
Engineering South (east of the OSU Edmon Low Library)
Agriculture Hall (corner of Monroe and Farm)
The Student Union Building
Note: These buildings will open up in the event that severe weather is imminent in the Stillwater area. Residents should arrive to these shelters in plenty of time before a warning is issued. Once a warning is issued, it is too late to get to a public shelter and do not drive to a public shelter once a warning is issued.

Sulphur:
Sulphur High School Saferoom – W. Ninth St. & Muskogee St. (Note: Handicapped assessable. Available to public during non-school hours).
City Maintenance Yard-2601 Public Works Drive.

Tulsa:
City-County Library

Tushka
Community shelter located underground at Tushka Public School

Warr Acres:
Outside City Hall - 5930 NW 49th
Cherokee Hills Park - NW 66th & Cherokee Dr.
Grandma's Park - NW 40th west of MacArthur

South Dakota

Abderdeen:

The No-Nonsense Guide To Tornado Safety

Avera St. Luke's Hospital-305 S. State St (use west side visitor's entrance).
Avera St. Luke's Hospital Midland Campus-1400 15th Ave. N.W., (open only through business hours, 8 a.m. to 5 p.m Weekdays).
Brown County Courthouse-25 Market St (Annex basement. Use doors on west side of courthouse annex or handicap entrance on north side of courthouse annex)
Federal Building (business hours only).
Frederick Area School, Main Street (use south doors. Available when severe weather warnings or watches are issued).
Groton High School-125 E. Fourth Ave. (use main entrance. Available when severe weather warnings or watches are issued).
Northern State University (hours: Other than school time, opened by security).
O.M. Tiffany School, 819 Eighth Ave. N.E. (use marked doors on Dakota Street entrance).

Irene:
Irene Community Center - 103 W. Main Street

Vermillion:
Vermillion Fire & EMS Station - 820 North Dakota Street
National Guard Armory - 603 Princeton Street

Wakonda:
Wakonda Public School - 212 Nebraska Street

Tennessee

Ardmore:
Ardmore City Hall-25844 Main St.

Dover:
Visitors Center-117 Visitor Center Lane

Franklin:
Franklin Recreational Complex-1120 Hillsboro Road (opens whenever threatening weather is possible).

La Vergne:
The Multipurpose Building (located behind City Hall)-5093 Murfreesboro Road (opens whenever threatening weather is possible).

Manchester:
Coffee County Middle School- 865 Mcminnville Hwy. (opens whenever threatening weather is possible).

Mt. Juliet:
First Baptist Church-735 N. Mount Juliet Road (opens whenever threatening weather is possible).

Nashville:
Donelson Fellowship- 3210 McGavock Pike (opens whenever threatening weather is possible).

Appendix F:

Tornado Research Pioneer Ted Fujita

Dr. Tetsuya Theodore "Ted" Fujita (1920-1998) was a pioneering researcher who has—almost unarguably—added more understanding to the library of knowledge and understanding of tornadoes (and severe storms) than anyone.

Among his noteworthy contributions to the field of meteorology is his introduction of the concept of "tornado families." Based on his extensive research and careful observations, Fujita correctly deduced—and later proved—that some tornado events were actually comprised of multiple and individual tornadoes, each with a unique path, but spawned by the same thunderstorm. Before this, lengthy damage paths were usually considered to be made by a single tornado. He also was responsible for introducing a great deal of the tornado terminology that is spoken in terms of general understanding today, such as the idea of a "wall cloud."

His research was also responsible for the revelation that some tornadoes were made up of multiple vortices. While this is generally known today, it was his research that first identified this fact by his examination of tornado damage patterns. This concept was confirmed subsequently by visually examining many videos of tornado funnels.

Perhaps his most enduring contribution to the understanding of tornadoes is the scale used to measure their relative power and strength—the "Fujita Scale" or tornado ratings. The scale was created and established by Fujita as a way of rating tornadoes by the extent of damage left behind as well as the estimated wind speeds of individual twisters.

After studying the 1974 "Super Tornado Outbreak," Fujita was able to identify new kind of windstorm. Based on his research, he identified two other wind-related weather phenomena that have become routinely reported (and understood) today; the *downburst* and the *microburst*. Before his research, meteorologists had not had a full understanding of confusing and destructive wind gust found in and around severe thunderstorms. This understanding evolved into means to distinguish tornado damage from damage of non-tornadic winds.

Without the contributions of Dr. Fujita, our understanding of tornadoes would no doubt be years behind where they currently are.

Index

The No-Nonsense Guide To Tornado Safety

References

"Basic Disaster Supplies Kit." Updated 5 September 2013 *Ready.gov* website. Retrieved 18 October 2013.

Bennett, Kevin. "Get to know storm shelters, officials urge" *American News* website. Retrieved 03 April 2013.

"Clay Clay Storm Shelter Locations." *Clay County Emergency Management Website*. Retrieved 10 April 2013.

"Communities offer unlocked public tornado shelters." 13 April 2012. *The Wichita Eagle* (Newspaper) Website. Retrieved 03 May 2012.

Corfidi, S., S. Weiss, J. Kain, S. Corfidi, R. Rabin, and J. Levit, 2010: Revisiting the 3–4 April 1974 "Super Outbreak of Tornadoes." Wea. Forecasting, 25, 465–510.

"Design Criteria for Tornado and Hurricane Safe Rooms" FEMA Publication P-361, pp-3.1 -3-24. Second Edition August 2008.

Doswell, C.A. III, H.E. Brooks, and N. Dotzek, 2009: "On the Implementation of the Enhanced Fujita Scale in the USA." Atmos. Res., 93, 554–563.

Draper, Robert. "The Last Chase." *National Geographic.* November 2013: 28-61. Print.

Edwards, R., and L.R. Lemon, 2002: Proactive or reactive? "The Severe Storm Threat to Large Event Venues." Preprints, 21st Conf. Severe Local Storms, San Antonio, Amer. Meteor. Soc.

Finger, Stan. "Harveyville Tornado Struck Without Warning, Weather Officials Say" *The Wichita Eagle* Published Friday, March 2, 2012.

Forbes, Greg, Dr. "Tornado Safety - Cars Versus Ditches: A Controversy." 11 May 2009. *Weather Channel* Website. Retrieved 29 April 2013.

The No-Nonsense Guide To Tornado Safety

"Frequently Asked Questions: Tornado/Hurricane Safe Rooms," Federal Emergency Management Agency (FEMA) Website. Updated 8 August 2013. Retreived 01 September 2013.

Grazulis, Thomas P The Tornado: Nature's Ultimate Windstorm. University of Oklahoma Press. 2001. Print.

Grazulis, Thomas P. "Tornado Myths". The Tornado: Nature's Ultimate Windstorm. University of Oklahoma Press. 2001. Print

Kis, A. K. and J. M. Straka, 2010: Nocturnal tornado climatology. Wea. Forecasting, 25, 545–561.

Lewellen, W.S., 1993: "Tornado vortex theory. The Tornado: Its Structure, Dynamics, Prediction, and Hazards "(C. Church, D. Burgess, C. Doswell, R. Davies-Jones, Eds.), Geophys. Monogr. 79, Amer. Geophys. Union, 19–39.

"Living In the 'Dixie Alley' Means Dangerous Tornadoes" March 16, 2012, WAFF News 48 Website. Retrieved October 18, 2013.

Mannette, Alice. "Oklahoma TV Weatherman Vilified for Tornado Advice." 31 May 2013 Chicago Tribune Website. Retrieved 10 August 2013.

Marsh, Patrick T. "A Review of NWS Tornado Emergencies," National Weather Service Instruction (NWSI),19 APRIL 2010 pp. 3-28

Mogil, Michael H. "Extreme Weather." Black Dog & Leviathan Publishers, Inc. 2007. Print.

"Norman Has Four Locations Designated as Public Storm Shelters" 14 April 2012 The Oklahoma Daily. The Oklahoma Daily Website. Retrieved 2 May 2013.

"Public Safe Room Initiatives." FEMA Website. Retrieved 26 April 2013.

"Public Storm Shelters." Stillwater, OK Government Website. Retrieved 01 May 2013.

"Public storm shelters announced in the Greater Oklahoma City Metro area (Photos)" 13 April 2012 Examiner.com. Retrieved 2 May 2013 from Public storm shelters announced in the Greater Oklahoma City Metro area (Photos).

Ray, P.S., P. Bieringer, X. Niu, and B. Whissel, 2003: An improved estimate of tornado occurrence in the central plains of the United States. Mon. Wea. Rev., 131, 1026–1031.

Rice, Dyole. "16-minute tornado warning saved lives." USAToday.com. 21 May 2013 Retrieved 15 April 2013

Rice, Doyle. "Dixie Alley May See More Tornado Action Than Even Tornado Alley." *USAToday.com* Date: 26 April 2011. Retrieved 15 April 2013.

Schneider, R.S., J.T. Schaefer, and H.E. Brooks, 2004: Tornado outbreak days: An updated and expanded climatology (1875–2003). Preprints, 22nd Conf. Severe Local Storms, Hyannis MA, P5.1.

"Severe Weather Shelters" *Kansas Turnpike Authority*. KTA Website. Retrieved 9 May 2013

Shaw, Alexis. "Should You Drive During A Tornado?" (1 June 21013). ABCNews.com. Retrieved 01 September 20132.

Sosnowski, Alex and AccuWeather.com (12 March 2012) "Can You Really Hide from a Tornado?" Scientific American. Retrieved 15 April 2013

Storm Prediction Center Online Tornado FAQ, Storm Prediction Center website, Updated 30 August 2013 Retrieved 16 April 2013

"Storm Shelters List." 4029tv.com Website. Retrieved 15 April 2013 from

"Storm Shelter Locations." *National Parks Service* Website. Retrieved 10 April 2013

"Tornado Safety." *Red Cross* website 2013 Retrieved September 30 2013

"Tornado Safety Rules for Schools," The Disaster Handbook 1998 National Edition, Institute of Food and Agricultural SciencesUniversity of Florida, p. 2

"Tornado Season, Part 2, Roars Into Action" *LiveScience* website. Retrieved 08 August 2013

"Tornado Shelters Being Built Across South, Midwest," *NBC News website*. 30 April 2013. Retrieved October 18, 2013

"Tornadoes," The Disaster Handbook 1998 National Edition, Institute of Food and Agricultural Sciences University of Florida. Print.

"Tornadoes." Talking About Disaster: Guide for Standard Messages. Pp 109 -129. National Disaster Education Coalition: American Red Cross, FEMA, IAEM, IBHS, NFPA, NWS, USDA/CSREES, and USGS.

"Tornado Warnings Are Too Often," Nov 02, 2010 *TerraDaily* website Retrieved 30 March 2013

"Tornadoes Numbers, Deaths, Injuries, and Adjusted Damage, 1950-1994," Retrieved 2 May 2013

The No-Nonsense Guide To Tornado Safety

"Where Are The Tornado Shelters Across Oklahoma?" 13 May 2012 KOCO TV website. Retrieved 1 May 2013

The No-Nonsense Guide To Tornado Safety

Cover Credits:
Wikipedia (http://en.wikipedia.org/wiki/Multiple-vortex_tornado)

Environmental Graffiti (http://www.environmentalgraffiti.com/meteorology/news-10-dangerous-tornado-myths-debunked)

Wikipedia (http://en.wikipedia.org/wiki/Tornadoes_of_2010)

Stormtrack.org. (http://www.stormtrack.org/forum/showthread.php?19834-What-exactly-is-the-Hook-Echo)

National Public Radio (http://www.npr.org/2011/06/17/137199914/advanced-tornado-technology-could-reduce-deaths)

p. 4
Wikipedia images (bow echo)

p. 5 tornado generation
https://www.toledoblade.com/State/2011/05/01/After-lethal-month-what-lies-ahead-2.html

P 8
Wikipedia images

P 9
http://smokeys-trail.com/tornado/1925.html

P. 10
NWS
http://www.srh.noaa.gov/srh/srnews/stories/2011/outbreak_smithvilleEF5.htm

p. 12
Wikipedia images (tornado alley)

The No-Nonsense Guide To Tornado Safety

p. 13
http://www.gpb.org/blogs/family/2013/01/30/severe-weather-safety-at-home#

p. 17
National Geographic (pp. 42-43). November 2013

P. 18
http://www.ncdc.noaa.gov/oa/climate/severeweather/tornadoes.html
NOAA

p. 18
http://www.wsaz.com/blogs/askjosh/45980227.htm

P. 20
Tornado safety
http://www.accuweather.com/en/weather-news/important-tornado-safety-tips-1/30770

P. 20
Important Tornado Safety Tips To Follow – AccuWeather
http://www.accuweather.com/en/weather-news/important-tornado-safety-tips-1/30770

p. 21
Insurance Institute for Business & Home Safety
http://www.disastersafety.org/tornado/reality-of-tornadoes_ibhs/
Living on Earth.org
http://www.loe.org/shows/segments.html?programID=06-P13-00024&segmentID=5

p. 23
Federal Emergency Management Agency (FEMA)
http://www.fema.gov/safe-rooms/wind-zones-united-states

p. 24
National Weather Service Weather Forecast Office/NOAA website, Jacksonville, FL.
http://www.srh.noaa.gov/jax/?n=tornadoes

p. 35
Tornado Safety – Weather Channel
http://www.weather.com/blog/weather/8_19417.html

The No-Nonsense Guide To Tornado Safety

Other Books in the No-Nonsense Safety Guide Series

Published By Lulu Books & Beyond The Spectrum

The No-Nonsense Guide To Tornado Safety

• Paperback: 84 pages • Publisher: lulu.com (November 22, 2013) • Language: English • ISBN-10: 1304648648 • ISBN-13: 978-1304648648 • Product Dimensions: 9 x 6 x 0.2 inches • Shipping Weight: 6.4 ounce

The No-Nonsense Guide To Blizzard Safety

• Paperback: 54 pages • Publisher: lulu.com (December 21, 2013) • Language: English • ISBN-10: 9781304709394 • Product Dimensions: 9 x 6 x 0.2 inches • Shipping Weight: 0.28 pounds

The No-Nonsense Guide To Flood Safety.

The No-Nonsense Guide To Tornado Safety

• Paperback: 60 pages • Publisher: lulu.com (November 22, 2013) • Language: English • ISBN-10: 1304648613 • Product Dimensions: 9 x 6 x 0.2 inches

The No-Nonsense Guide To Hurricane Safety.

• Paperback: 59 pages • Publisher: lulu.com (December 20, 2013) • Language: English • ISBN-10: 9781304733030 • Product Dimensions: 9 x 6 x 0.2 inches

Other upcoming books in the series include: "The No-Nonsense Guide to Fire Safety," The No-Nonsense Guide To Earthquake Safety," and "The No-Nonsense Guide To Automobile Safety."

www.ingramcontent.com/pod-product-compliance
Lightning Source LLC
Chambersburg PA
CBHW020341290526
45785CB00005B/2120